MAXIMISE YOUR MARK

graphic products
revision guide

TRISTRAM SHEPARD

Published in 2004 by:
Nelson Thornes Ltd
Delta Place
27 Bath Road
CHELTENHAM
GL53 7TH
United Kingdom

06 07 08 / 10 9 8 7 6 5 4 3 2

A catalogue record for this book is available from the British Library

ISBN 0 7487 8994 4

Illustrations by Tristram Ariss, Hardlines and Tristram Shepard
Page make-up by Turchini Design, London
Picture research by Sue Sharp

Printed and bound in Croatia by Zrinski

Acknowledgements
Special thanks are due to Russ Jones for his detailed comments and suggestions.
The publishers are grateful to the following for permission to reproduce photographs
or other illustrative material:

Advertising Archives (p 21 left)
Art Directors & TRIP Photo Library (p 6, p 30 right, p 49 bottom right)
Cadbury's (p4 5 bottom)
Centre for Rapid Prototyping in Manufacturing, University of Nottingham
(p 42 middle left)
Corel Corporation (p 15 centre, p 29 centre, p 36 left, p 37 middle, p 45 top, p 47
middle and bottom, p 50 top and bottom, p 55 top and middle right, p 56 lower middle
and bottom left, p 57 bottom right, p 62 left)
Denford Ltd (p 42 top)
Dorling Kindersley (p 25 bottom left)
Dyson (p 15 bottom left)
Ecover (p 37 bottom)
Getty Telegraph Colour Library (p 44 bottom left)
Hallmark (p 51 bottom)
Hemera Technologies Inc. (p 4, p 5 top and bottom, p 7, p 9, p 15 top and bottom
right, p 16, p 17, p 18, p 19 top, p 21 top right, middle and bottom, p 22, p 24 left and
bottom, p 25 top right, middle and bottom, p 27, p 29 top right and bottom left, p 30
left, p 31, p 32, p 33, p 34, p 35 top and middle, p 36 top, centre and bottom, p 37
top, p 38, p 39 bottom, p 40, p 41, p 42 bottom right, p 43 lower middle and bottom,
p 44 top, centre and bottom, p 47 top left, p 48, p 49, p 54 top, p 56 lower middle and
bottom, p 57 top left and bottom left, p 58 top right, p 60 top right, p 61 middle right,
p 63 top &and lower middle)
Macromedia (p 23)
Martin Sookias / Universal Coatings (p 58 middle, p 61 left)
Martyn F Chillmaid (front cover, p 35 bottom right, p 45 bottom right, p 50 middle
centre, p 53 top, The Elements of Pop Up, p 55 left and bottom left, p 57 top right,
p 60 left, p 61 bottom)
Nokia (p 20 bottom left, p 42 bottom left)
Published and designed by 'Child's Play' (p 59 top)
Powerstock / Zefa (p5 0 bottom left)
Quark Inc. (p 28)
Royal Mail (p 56 middle right)
Simon Phillips (p 23 top)
Science Photo Library: Deep Light Productions (p 52 top)
Techsoft UK Ltd (p 20 bottom right)
Tristram Shepard (p 8)

Contents

Introduction   4

Improve Your Technique   5

Revision Planning Charts   10

Study Guide Topic 1   15
Materials and Components

Study Guide Topic 2   20
Design and Market Influences (1)

Study Guide Topic 3   25
Design and Market Influences (2)

Study Guide Topic 4   30
Evaluating Products and Applications

Study Guide Topic 5   35
Design Issues

Study Guide Topic 6   40
Using ICT

Study Guide Topic 7   45
Health and Safety

Study Guide Topic 8   50
Systems and Control

Study Guide Topic 9   55
Industrial Practice (1)

Study Guide Topic 10   60
Industrial Practice (2)

Introduction

Maximise Your Mark has been developed to help make revision for the GCSE written paper more worthwhile, and more enjoyable. It provides a comprehensive, structured programme of study and revision that helps you identify what you know and don't know. The first section also gives you tips on the best ways to tackle questions.

There are a number of ways in which you might use this book:

● as a weekly programme of study during the final year of your GCSE course

● as a revision checklist to work through in the months just before you take the written paper.

The book is divided up into ten topics that cover the examination specification. Each topic has five sections. Each section is contained on a single page and includes an example question for you to try. Most sections also include a handy cross-reference to pages in the GCSE *Design & Make It! Graphic Products* textbook, where you will find more details. Keywords and relevant web-links are provided, where appropriate.

A CD-Rom version of this book may be available in your school. Ask your teacher if it is on your school's network, or on any stand-alone PCs, and if there are copies of the CDs you can purchase for home use. The electronic version also includes animated illustrations, multiple-choice questions, sample answers with examiners' comments and a full glossary.

The Design & Make It! team hope that *Maximise Your Mark: Graphic Products Revision Guide* will help you get the marks you deserve in your written paper.

Good luck in your exams!

Tristram Shepard
Series editor

Improve Your Technique

Did you know that doing well in your Design & Technology written paper involves more than just knowing all the information contained in this study guide? You also need to know how to tackle the particular types of questions you will be asked – what the examiner is going to be looking for, how long to spend on each answer, how to approach sketching, etc.

The study and revision techniques you are learning in your other subjects are going to be very useful with D&T too, but the D&T written papers are a little bit different from most of the others that you sit. The next few pages are intended to help focus your revision on exactly what's required for the Graphic Products examination.

Top Tips

Here are six top tips to help you maximise your mark:

1 Read the question very carefully
2 Look closely at the available marks for each part of the question
3 Use the marks as a guide to how long you should spend on each question
4 Use Graphic Products keywords and phrases whenever possible
5 Use clear, neat rough sketches
6 Remember to use your coursework

1 Read the question very carefully

Sounds obvious doesn't it? However, many students throw marks away simply because they've not paused for a moment and checked what's really being asked for. It's all too easy to spot a couple of familiar words in a question and start writing everything you know about them. No D&T question ever works like this!

Each question is asking you to show and apply your knowledge in some way. For example, you may need to:

● discuss the advantages and disadvantages of...
● provide a number of examples of...
● explain what is meant by a specific term when used in a particular situation...

- Advantages and disadvantages
- Analyse
- Calculate
- Compare (and contrast)
- Describe
- Detail
- Develop
- Differences (and similarities)
- Draw
- Evaluate
- Give reasons
- Identify
- Label
- List
- Name
- Outline
- State
- Study
- Use notes and sketches

On the left are some other words commonly used in questions – you need to be clear on what each is instructing you to do.

When the examiner comes to mark your paper he or she has to follow a set mark scheme that matches the specific requirements of each question. So if there are two marks for giving two advantages and two marks for giving two disadvantages, you can only score a maximum of half-marks if you only discuss the advantages – however many you cover. In a similar way, you'll lose marks if you fail to provide the correct number of examples required.

2 Look closely at the available marks for each part of the question

To make life a bit easier, the D&T written papers give you plenty of information about how many marks are available for each part of each question. In some cases it might even show you that there are, say, two marks for stating the advantages and two for the disadvantages. In another it might be a little less obvious, but it's usually quite easy to work out what the marking scheme is going to be. For example, what do you think the marking scheme for the following question is likely to be?

> Explain two differences between thermosetting plastics and thermoplastics, giving an example of each. *(6 marks)*

Here you are being asked for two examples, which are likely to be allocated a mark each. That leaves four marks for the explanation of the two differences, i.e. two marks for each difference. These two marks are likely to be subdivided, with one mark for identifying a suitable difference, and the other for the quality of explanation you provide.

You need to get into the habit of providing examples and explanations. Unless the question asks for a list, it's unlikely that a simple one word answer is going to be enough to get you the marks. Basically for each section you study or revise you can pre-prepare a number of examples or explanations, and then use whichever supports the answer to the question most effectively.

During your course you should get to know the names of some designers and things that have been designed. Try to use specific examples in which you name the names of the designer, product model and/or manufacturer. So instead of just saying an 'MP3 player' you might write 'the Apple MP3 iPod, designed by Jonathan Ive', or 'the Cyclone cleaner, designed by James Dyson', instead of just 'a vacuum cleaner'. Examples like these will quickly earn the marks.

3 Use the marks as a guide to how long you should spend on each question

In the D&T written papers there's a very simple guide as to how long to spend on each question – a mark a minute! So if a question is worth six marks you should be spending around five or six minutes attempting to answer it. If it only takes you, say, one minute, then it's possible that you haven't provided enough detail. If the six minutes is nearly up and you're only halfway through, then you're probably writing far too much.

Remember that you'll need to include some initial time to read the question and think about your answer – don't just start writing. Start by checking the mark scheme, working out what examples you are going to use, thinking of the appropriate technical terms, etc.

Getting the timing right on longer questions that ask you to sketch and develop ideas is rather more difficult. It's very important that you practise answering these sorts of questions in the appropriate amount of time before the final examination. Again use the breakdown of the amount of marks as a guide. If there are, say, 15 marks to sketch three ideas, and 20 marks to develop one in more detail, make sure you spend about 15 minutes on the initial sketches and 20 minutes on the more detailed drawing. There is more advice on sketching on page 8.

With D&T papers you are advised to attempt the answer the questions in the order in which they are set. This is because the answer to one may lead on to the answer to a following question. However, it's still important not to spend too much time on a question you are finding difficult. Do what you can in the given time, and then move on. If there's time left at the end you can then go back and try to finish it off.

4 Use Graphic Products keywords and phrases whenever possible

On each page of the study guides that follow you'll find a number of keywords. You need to know what each one means and how to use it correctly in a sentence. You will find that you already know what many of them mean, which is just as well as in all there are about two hundred! Whenever you come across a word or phrase you are not familiar with, make a point of finding out what it means – ask your teacher or look it up in a textbook. If your school has the *Maximise Your Mark: Graphic Products* CD-Rom you can check the glossary, or use the QuickSearch option.

Aim to use as many of these keyword terms as possible in your written paper: they really help show that you know what you're talking about. In many questions each one you use might easily earn you an extra mark, and make the difference between one grade and another.

It's also a good idea to try and remember the group of keywords that apply to each section. When you come across a question that relates to that section, thinking of as many keywords as possible will help you recall what it's all about. For example, here's a group of keywords:

● ICT (Information and Communication Technology)
● CAD (Computer Aided Design)
● CAM (Computer Aided Manufacture)
● CNC (Computer Numerical Control)

Suppose a question comes up about the use of CAD. If you have learnt the whole group of keywords it will help you quickly recall a much wider range of information about CAD, and you might also be able to use some of the other keywords in your answer.

5 Use clear, neat rough sketches

Despite being called a 'written' paper, you will probably find you have to do some sketching. In fact you may find a series of related questions that ask you to generate and develop a design idea using sketches. These questions might take you nearly an hour, and be worth half the marks of the whole paper. Learning how to tackle these sorts of questions is therefore essential if you are going to get a good grade: make sure you do plenty of practice questions like these before the final paper.

In the examination you are not expected to do measured drawings, i.e. using a ruler. This is mainly because it would take too long. In doing your coursework you should have developed the ability to use clear, neat rough sketches – and these are exactly what are required here. Remember to add notes to your drawings to help explain your thoughts – these might help explain your thinking, e.g. 'This shape will be easy to vacuum form', or may be problems you are considering, e.g. ' What would be the best way to join these pieces together?' You can also use words to help describe a shape or form you are finding difficult to sketch.

Avoid adding colour to your sketches (unless of course the question specifically asks you to do so), and only use it sparingly for emphasis.

As always, make sure you read the question carefully and are covering exactly what is asked for in terms of the number of drawings, whether notes and evaluations are needed, or particular types of drawings, e.g. plans, elevations, 3D, etc. If it's up to you, then choose 2D views as they are easier and quicker to complete.

On the next page are examples of a very successful response to a series of shorter questions, worth about half the total marks for the paper! Could you do something similar in the exam in about an hour?

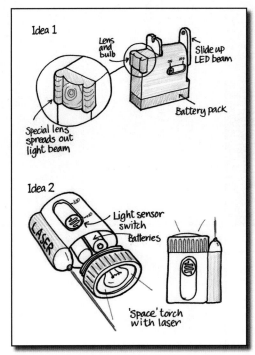

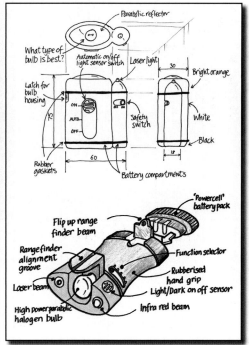

6 Remember to use your coursework

Sometimes questions ask you to refer to your GCSE coursework, perhaps as an example. Be aware that the person marking your written paper will not have seen your practical work or design folder, so you will probably need to give some brief information about what you designed and made.

You may find it helpful to think back to your coursework. For example, if you need to give an example of something designed for batch production, or maybe to explain the process of vacuum-forming, the work you did during your course might help remind you of the key points.

Other questions might show you a photograph of a product and ask you to develop its specification, or undertake an analysis and evaluation of it. You will have probably done similar exercises during your course. Although the product might be slightly different, think back to the sort of observations you made, and see if they apply to this example.

Finally, remember that the examination is trying to find out what you *do* know and understand, not what you don't. We all hope you manage to Maximise Your Mark!

MAXIMISE YOUR MARK

Graphic Products

Topic 1	Materials and Components	Topic / Section Start Date	Target Finish Date	Actual Finish Date	How well did I do on the written paper question? How could I have maximised my marks? — End of Topic Review ✓	What do I need to revise again for this section?
Section 1	Physical properties					
Section 2	Finishing off					
Section 3	Cutting and joining					
Section 4	Different drawing media					
Section 5	Drawing tools					
Topic 2	Design and Market Influences (1)				End of Topic Review ✓	
Section 1	Purpose and audience					
Section 2	Promoting a product					
Section 3	Sketching ideas in 2D and 3D					
Section 4	Making it look real					
Section 5	Designing with colour					

MAXIMISE YOUR MARK

Graphic Products

Topic / Section	Topic / Section Start Date	Target Finish Date	Actual Finish Date	End of Topic Review ✓	How well did I do on the written paper question? How could I have maximised my marks?	What do I need to revise again for this section?
Topic 3 Design and Market Influences (2)						
Section 1 Presentation media and materials						
Section 2 Pictorial drawings						
Section 3 Working drawings						
Section 4 Surface developments (nets)						
Section 5 Information drawings						
Topic 4 Evaluating Products and Applications				End of Topic Review ✓		
Section 1 The quality of design and manufacture						
Section 2 Investigating needs and wants						
Section 3 Performance requirements						
Section 4 Testing and evaluation by designers						
Section 5 Testing and evaluation by other people						

11

MAXIMISE YOUR MARK

Graphic Products

Revision Planner

Name _____   **Form** _____

Topic / Section Start Date	Target Finish Date	Actual Finish Date	How well did I do on the written paper question? How could I have maximised my marks?	What do I need to revise again for this section?	End of Topic Review ✓
Topic 5 Design Issues					
Section 1 Social, cultural and moral issues					
Section 2 Environmental issues					
Section 3 The 3 Rs					
Section 4 Packaging and the environment					
Section 5 Environmental graphics					
Topic 6 Using ICT					End of Topic Review ✓
Section 1 CAD/CAM Systems					
Section 2 2D CAD programs					
Section 3 3D CAD programs					
Section 4 Sharing electronic data					
Section 5 The advantages and disadvantages of using CAD/CAM					

MAXIMISE YOUR MARK

Revision Planner

Name _____   **Form** _____

Graphic Products

	Topic / Section Start Date	Target Finish Date	Actual Finish Date	How well did I do on the written paper question? How could I have maximised my marks?	What do I need to revise again for this section?
Topic 7 Health and Safety				End of Topic Review ✓	
Section 1 Consumer information					
Section 2 Quality Assurance					
Section 3 Hazards and risks					
Section 4 Controlling risk					
Section 5 A safe working environment					
Topic 8 Systems and Control				End of Topic Review ✓	
Section 1 System breakdown					
Section 2 System flow charts					
Section 3 Registration marks and colour bars					
Section 4 Simple mechanisms					
Section 5 Complex mechanisms					

MAXIMISE YOUR MARK

Graphic Products

	Topic / Section Start Date	Target Finish Date	Actual Finish Date	End of Topic Review ✓	
				How well did I do on the written paper question? How could I have maximised my marks?	What do I need to revise again for this section?
Topic 9 Industrial Practice (1)					
Section 1 Making things in quantity					
Section 2 Commercial printing methods					
Section 3 Process colours					
Section 4 Special effects					
Section 5 Cutting and folding tools					
Topic 10 Industrial Practice (2)				End of Topic Review ✓	
Section 1 Packaging matters					
Section 2 Barcode scanning					
Section 3 Units of paper and card					
Section 4 Reducing waste					
Section 5 Using patterns, templates and jigs					

Physical Properties

Designers need to decide about the flexibility, finish, rigidity, strength, quality, weight and cost of the materials they specify.

The **physical properties** of a material describe its qualities, e.g. strong, light, smooth, etc. The **performance characteristics** describe how the material is likely to behave while being worked on, or changed in some way, e.g. cut, bent, heated, etc.

Paper and Board

In graphic products, paper-based materials tend to be chosen for their strength, resistance to tear, weight, ability to take printing inks and to survive automatic bonding and shaping equipment. There is a wide range of different types of paper and card, including cartridge, layout, tracing and corrugated.

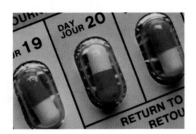

Plastics

Plastics, such as acetate, polyethylenes, polystyrenes and PVC, are used in packaging and other graphic products. Plastics need to be suitable for shaping and forming, e.g. moulded expanded polystyrene, blister packs, bubble wrap, etc.

Modelling Materials

A wide variety of materials can be used to create **prototypes** and **presentation models**. Some of the most common materials used are:

- corrugated plastic sheet
- block foam
- mouldable materials
- foam core board
- hard wax

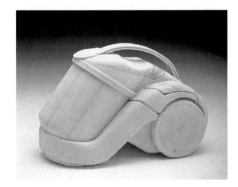

The materials chosen for a model will often have very different properties from the material being represented. For example, card can be a very useful, cheap and easy to work substitute for sheet metal. The ways in which card can be shaped (e.g. cut and bent) are in many ways similar to sheet metal.

Written Question

Answer the following question on plain or lined paper.
Do not spend more than 10 minutes writing your answer.

A manufacturer needs to produce a package for a chocolate Easter Egg. The packaging materials will include folded card and silver foil. Say what particular properties these two materials have, and explain why they will be particularly suitable for this type of package. *(8 marks)*

Finishing Off

Finishes

Most materials need to have some form of **finish** applied to them. This adds to their properties by making them stronger, water- or paint-resistant, more durable, more attractive, etc.

Sometimes materials need to be **prepared** first so that they will take the finish well. The surfaces of resistant materials can then be stained, polished or painted, and given a plastic-based finish to add an attractive, shiny and tough outer layer of protection.

A surfboard needs a good water-resistant finish

Paint and Ink

Paint and **ink** are frequently applied to the surfaces of graphic products. Inks are made from a solid colour **pigment** mixed with a liquid **vehicle**. The vehicle can be water-based, water-soluble or solvent-based. The mixture of pigment to vehicle affects the quality of the finish. It needs to be matched to the absorption properties of the surfaces of paper and board it is to be applied to. This prevents ink 'bleeding' through or 'pooling' on the surface.

Smart New Finishes

Modern manufacturing technologies are creating exciting new finishes for paper and boards. For example, the finish on ink-jet papers can provide a very high quality of photographic reproduction. Gold, silver, and textured surfaces can be applied. Special new inks can change colour when a small amount of heat is applied. These are known as **smart materials**.

Fixing and Filling

Some graphic media (e.g. pastels and chalks) require **fixing** with a fixative spray to prevent smudging and to help protect the surface.

When making **presentation models** from block modelling materials, small holes and gaps tend to occur where different materials are joined together. These need to be '**filled**' in some way, using body filler, plaster, etc. After they have been **sealed** they can be finished using acrylic, cellulose or water-based paints.

Here's what you need to know...

about various ways in which finishes can be added to materials. This includes adding colour and graphics to card.

See *Design & Make It! Graphic Products* Revised pages 71, 76–77 (63, 68–69 earlier edition).

KEYWORDS
Do you know what the following terms mean?
● Finish
● Pigment
● Vehicle
● Smart materials
● Fixing
● Presentation models

Presentation models need to be very carefully finished if they are to look realistic

---

Written Question

Answer the following questions on plain or lined paper.
Do not spend more than 5 minutes writing your answers.

i) Explain briefly why most materials need to have some form of finish applied to them. *(2 marks)*

ii) Presentation models made from block modelling materials usually need to be filled. Explain what is meant by the term 'filled'. *(2 marks)*

iii) After being filled, presentation models are usually finished. Give two examples of suitable finishes that might be applied. *(2 marks)*

Cutting and Joining

Cutting Tools

The most common cutting tools for paper and board materials are craft knives, scissors and rotary cutters. More specialised tools such as fret saws and die cutters are also used.

The cutting tool needs to be right for the job. It depends on things like the length, depth and accuracy of cut required. As always, using these tools **safely** is very important – all cutting tools have very sharp blades.

Here's what you need to know...

about how different materials used in graphic products can be cut and fixed together.

KEYWORDS
Do you know what the following terms mean?
● Adhesives
● Polyvinyl acetate (PVA)

Adhesives

Graphic materials can be fixed together using a variety of **adhesives**. Some form a bond immediately (known as **contact adhesives**), while others permit some adjustment before they harden. For thin paper, adhesive tapes and rubber-solution ('cow' gum) are best as they do not distort the paper or leave marks. **Spray adhesives** are very effective for fixing artwork and photos to card, but they are expensive and must only be used in properly ventilated areas. **PVA (polyvinyl**

acetate) is a good all-purpose adhesive for thick paper and card, though, if available, a **hot melt glue** gun is a very efficient method.

When using adhesives it is always very important to choose the most appropriate one. Safety is also an important consideration: consider the potential hazards and minimise the risks involved. For example, if not used carefully a hot melt glue gun can spoil the appearance of the material and cause burns and blisters.

Fixings

When making 3D graphic products, such as models or packages, ready-made **fixings** can be used to join materials together. For example, paper-clips, fasteners, staples, 'poppers', etc.

Remember, the way a graphic product is cut and fixed together in a batch or mass-production process may be different from the way it is done as a one-off in a school workshop.

Written Questions

Answer the following questions on plain or lined paper.
Do not spend more than 5 minutes writing your answers.

1   Study the photograph of a cardboard theatre on the right.
   i)   Name one suitable tool that could be used to cut the material out, and another tool that would aid the safe and accurate use of the first tool. *(2 marks)*
   ii) Name one suitable adhesive that could be used to stick the sides of the product together. *(1 mark)*

2   Explain two potential hazards when using a hot melt glue gun. *(4 marks)*

Different Drawing Media

Rendering

There are lots of materials and tools that can be used to make marks on a surface. Each gives a different effect. Designers need to choose the one that most effectively communicates the shape, form and material being represented. This process of adding **colour** and **texture** to a drawing to make it look like more like a material is called **rendering**.

2D CAD 'Draw' and **'Paint'** programs have a wide range of tools for rendering colours and textured surfaces. Images created on-screen can be printed out or sent electronically.

Pencils

Pencils can be graphite (black) or coloured. Hard pencils are used to create accurate plans and **working drawings**. Softer pencils are ideal for quick sketches. Variations of tone and texture can be easily created.

Felt Markers

Felt markers are good for showing large flat areas of colour, particularly if the material being represented is smooth, such as plastic or metal. It is difficult to alter or remove a mark made with a felt pen.

Technical Pens

Technical pens that produce fine ink lines are best for accurate plans and workshop drawings. They produce a much blacker line than a hard pencil, but are more difficult to correct.

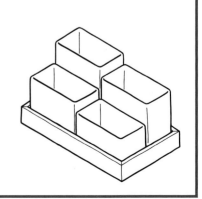

Paints

Paints come in a wide variety of different types, from powder to watercolour, acrylic and oil-based. Water-based paints are less thick and can be more easily mixed and **blended** on a paper surface. Acrylic and oil-based paints are much brighter and suitable for applying to a wide range of hard surfaces.

Chalks and Pastels

Chalks and pastels are quick and easy to use. They are particularly good at adding tone and shading as they can be quickly blended and **graduated**. They can also be used effectively on coloured paper or board backgrounds.

Here's what you need to know...

about graphic media.

See *Design & Make It! Graphic Products* Revised pages 112–115 (104–107 earlier edition).

KEYWORDS
Do you know what the following terms mean?
● Render
● Working drawings
● Blend
● Graduation

WWW.
Go to:
www.berol.co.uk
www.daler-rowney.co.uk
www.faber-castell.com
www.winsornewton.com

Written Question

Answer the following question on plain white paper.
Do not spend more than 15 minutes on your answer.

On the right is a line drawing of a desk-tidy. The sides are made from hard shiny acrylic and the base is made from untreated wood.

i) Using drawing instruments, make an accurate copy of the line drawing on plain white paper. *(5 marks)*

ii) Use pencils, technical pens, felt pens and/or paints to add colour. Use different media to show the plastic and wooden surfaces. *(10 marks)*

Drawing Equipment

To create high quality drawings, designers often need to choose which tools and equipment will be best for the job. These include:

- drawing boards
- set squares
- CAD software
- T squares and rulers
- compasses and dividers

French Curves

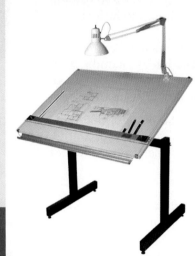

Drawing Boards

Drawing boards are used to provide a flat, clean surface. Paper needs to be held in position on the board using board clips, masking tape, or some other means.

T Squares and Rulers

T squares, or parallel bars help ensure horizontal lines and vertical lines are drawn at exactly 90°. Rulers help provide accurate measurements. They need to be used with T squares, or set squares, and dividers.

Set Squares

Set squares come in two main types – 45° and 30/60°. Use a 45° set square for **planometric drawings** and a 30/60° set square for **isometric drawings**. They need to be used in conjunction with T squares.

Compasses and Dividers

Compasses help draw accurate circles. Dividers are used as a measuring tool.

2D and 3D CAD

2D and **3D CAD** can be used to create complex line drawings. These drawings can then be printed, or even sent directly to a cutting machine.

Written Question

Answer the following question on plain or lined paper.
Do not spend more than 5 minutes writing your answer.

You have been asked to accurately draw a cube with sides 150mm long in isometric projection on a plain piece of A3 paper. State three drawing tools you would use, and explain the purpose of each. *(6 marks)*

Purpose and Audience

A great idea for a new product can be worthless unless:

- the client can see and be convinced that the product will sell well.
- the manufacturer can understand how the product needs to be made.
- the consumer realises the **features and benefits** the product has, and wants to purchase it.

To achieve these things designers need to present their proposals carefully. The **client**, **manufacturer** and **consumer** all want different information about the product, presented in different ways. Designers need to think about:

- the **purpose** of the presentation (i.e. what information they need to communicate), and
- the **audience** (who they are communicating to).

The Client

The client wants to check that the features, appearance and selling price of the product match the current demands of potential customers. Research data needs to be presented as easy-to-read **graphs** and **charts**. The product's features and appearance can be shown as coloured drawings, **mock-ups**, working **prototypes** and/or **presentation models**.

The Manufacturer

The manufacturer wants to know about the materials, sizes, components and manufacturing processes involved. This information needs to be communicated through accurate **technical drawings** and material specifications.

The Consumer

The consumer wants to know what the product does, what benefits it will bring, how much it costs and from where it can be obtained. This information will be in the form of attractive **advertisements**, sales leaflets, publicity stunts, etc.

Using ICT

ICT could be extensively used to communicate design ideas to different audiences using **virtual prototypes**, on-screen presentations, **CAD** systems, etc.

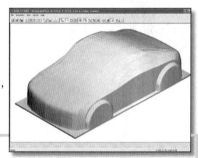

Here's what you need to know...

about communicating design ideas in different ways to clients, manufacturers and potential customers.

See *Design & Make It! Graphic Products* Revised pages 121–122, 134–135, 139–143 (113–114, 126–127, 131–135 earlier edition).

KEYWORDS
Do you know what the following terms mean?
- Features and benefits
- Client
- Manufacturer
- Consumer
- Purpose and audience
- Graphs and charts
- Mock-up
- Prototype
- Presentation model
- Technical drawings
- Advertisements
- ICT
- Virtual prototype
- CAD

Written Question

Answer the following question on plain or lined paper.
Do not spend more than 5 minutes writing your answer.

A design team has developed the casing for a new mobile phone aimed at teenagers. They now need to present their ideas to:
i)   a mobile phone company (the client)
ii) a manufacturer
iii) potential customers.

For each of the above suggest a suitable use of ICT and briefly explain what information it would help communicate.   (*6 marks*)

Promoting a Product

Advertising Matters

Advertising is essential, particularly when a new product is launched. If people don't know the product is available they can't be expected to buy it! When they become aware of a new product people then need to be informed about what it does (its **features**) and why they might need or want it (its **benefits**).

Finding a Gap in the Market

Not everyone wants the same thing. Different products appeal to different people. Most products are designed for a particular group of people. Companies look for a '**gap in the market**' to make a product for (i.e. a product that is not currently available aimed at a particular market that will want it). For example, a sportswear company might identify a need for a range of lower-cost and lower-performance shoes for a particular sporting activity that young children are becoming interested in.

Target Marketing

Advertising is expensive so it needs to be targeted at the people most likely to want the product. This is known as **target marketing**. The advertisements will be placed where the target market is most likely to see them. For example:

● in specialist magazines.
● during TV programmes they are most likely to watch.
● at places and events they are most likely to attend.
● alongside other products they are likely to purchase.

Lifestyle

The images and words used in advertising materials need to reflect the **lifestyles** of the target market. For example:

● showing the product being used in places and situations the target market might want to be.
● showing the product being used by 'celebrities' who the target market identify with.
● using words and phrases that the target market might use.
● suggesting features and benefits that will particularly appeal to the target market.

Written Question

Answer the following question on plain or lined paper. Do not spend more than about 10 minutes writing your answer.

You have been asked to suggest an appropriate method of advertising a new bar of soap aimed at male and female users in the 15–25 age range. The product is part of an 'environmentally friendly' product range. This is the main benefit of the soap.

Suggest:
i) a suitable magazine in which to place a full-page colour advertisement.
ii) a suitable TV programme during which to show a 15 second advertisement.
iii) a suitable celebrity to endorse the product.
iv) a suitable location and/or event to present the product.
v) two suitable descriptive words that might be used in an advertisement.

Give reasons for each of your choices. *(10 marks)*

Sketching Ideas in 2D and 3D

**Here's what you
need to know...**

about using freehand
drawings to sketch
ideas in 2D and 3D.

See *Design & Make It!
Graphic Products*
Revised pages
108–111, 118–119,
130–131 (100–103,
110–111, 122–123
earlier edition).

KEYWORDS
Do you know what the
following terms mean?
● Sketch
● Annotation
● Plan
● Elevations
● Orthographic
  projection
● Two-dimensional
  (2D)
● Three-dimensional
  (3D)
● Isometric drawing
● Perspective
● Crating
● Wire-frame model
● Scale
● Cut-away drawings
● Exploded drawings

Using Sketches

When designers are coming up with new ideas
they make quick **sketches** of them on paper.
Sometimes they find it difficult to keep up – the
ideas flow quicker than they can sketch. There
certainly isn't time to use rulers, technical
drawing aids or a computer! These sketches can
then be shown to, and discussed with, other
members of the design team.

Adding Labels

Another way to speed up the process of recording an idea on paper is to use
annotations, or 'labels' alongside a sketch. For example, it might be quicker to label
part of a product sketch with the words 'dark green', than it is to find the right
shade of pencil or felt-pen to colour it in. As well as words, numbers can be added
to indicate quantities, sizes, etc.

2D Freehand Drawing Techniques

Designers use a variety of methods to show the product they are sketching. They
might sketch a **plan** or an **elevation**, or both together (i.e. a rough **orthographic
projection**). These are **2D** freehand drawing techniques.

3D Freehand Drawing Techniques

Alternatively, designers might use **3D** freehand drawing techniques, using simple
isometric or **perspective** projections. These are more difficult, so they use the
method of '**crating**'. This involves sketching a rectangular box and fitting the
product being sketched inside it. Curved shapes and forms can be contained in a
'crate'. Another approach is to use a **wire-frame model**. Specially printed grid-
paper can be used as an underlay to make construction of 3D sketches easier.

Other Freehand Drawing Techniques

Remember, it is not always necessary to sketch the whole product each time.
Designers often focus on one part of the product and just sketch that. They may
sketch the part much larger than it will be in reality, i.e. change its **scale**. Other
techniques they use include '**cut-away**' sketches and '**exploded**' sketches.

Written Question

Answer the following question on plain paper.
Do not spend more than 20 minutes drawing
your answer.

You have been asked to sketch some initial design
ideas for a new torch. It is to be used as a 'prop' in a
science fiction film set in the near future.

Produce at least two annotated sketches that show
the development of one idea. Include at least two of
the following techniques:
• an orthographic freehand drawing (2D plan and
  elevations).
• a 3D freehand drawing (isometric or
  perspective).
• a freehand drawing showing a detail.
• a cut-away or exploded freehand drawing.

As you sketch your ideas you should include notes
about:
• how the torch will be held.
• how it will be switched on and off.
• what shape and size of bulb will be used.
• how the source of power can be replenished.
• the materials that might be used, and how it
  might be made.

Note that marks will be
awarded primarily for the
appropriate use and quality
of your sketching and the
techniques you use, rather
than for the product you
design.   *(20 marks)*

Making it Look Real

After the outline drawing of a product has been created designers add **colour** and **texture** to make it look more like the real thing. This is known as 'enhancement', or '**rendering**'. Some drawings can be so realistic they look just like photographs.

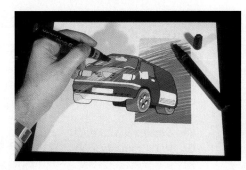

Here's what you need to know...

about adding realism to drawings through colour and texture.

See *Design & Make It! Graphic Products* Revised pages 112–115 (104–107 earlier edition).

KEYWORDS
Do you know what the following terms mean?
● Rendering
● Component
● Hatching
● Three-dimensional (3D)

WWW.
Go to:
www.berol.co.uk
www.daler-rowney.co.uk
www.faber-castell.com
www.windsornewton.com

Using Lines

Designers use pencils, pens, chalks, paint and other tools to help make drawings of products look more realistic. Using a different thickness of line can help make a form look more solid, or add emphasis to a particular **component**. **Hatching** can also be used to indicate different surfaces and materials.

Adding **highlights** and **shading** to indicate dark and light areas helps the representation of a **three-dimensional (3D)** form.

Making Marks

Different graphic marks can help show the surface texture of the material an object is made from, such as wood, metal or plastic. These can be shown to be smooth and shiny or perhaps hard and rough, or even reflective or transparent.

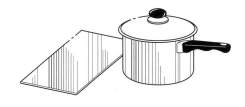

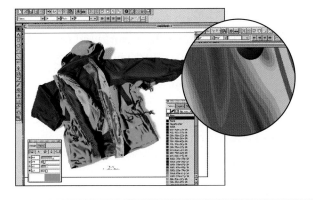

On the Computer

Drawings created using a '**Draw**' or '**Paint**' type program on a computer can be rendered in similar ways. Some programs have special filters and tools to create highly sophisticated representations of form and texture. These are not easy to create, but can be quick to experiment with and adjust in order to achieve the effect required.

Written Question

Answer the following questions on plain paper. You will need to copy them on to paper first.
Do not spend more than 20 minutes completing your answers.

a) On the right are outline drawings of three cubes. Use a variety of media and techniques to enhance each one as follows:
   i)   to look as if it were made from wood.
   ii) to look as if it were made from concrete.
   iii) to look as if it were made from transparent acrylic.
   (18 marks)

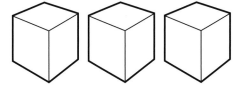

b) Imagine you are going to use a computer to undertake the same exercise. Name the main type of program you will use. *(2 marks)*

Here's what you need to know...

about designing with colour.

See *Design & Make It! Graphic Products* Revised pages 32–35, 75 (24–27, 67 earlier edition).

KEYWORDS
Do you know what the following terms mean?
- Primary colours
- Secondary colours
- Colour wheel
- Colour circle
- Harmonious colours
- Complementary colours
- Contrast
- Hue
- Colour scheme
- Colour association
- Colour fusion
- Colour separation

Designing with Colour

Primary and Secondary Colours

The three **primary colours** are red, yellow and blue. When mixed together in pairs they produce the three **secondary colours** as follows:

red + yellow = orange   **red + blue = purple**   **yellow + blue = green**

The Colour Wheel

The primary and secondary colours can be shown together on what is known as the **colour wheel** or **colour circle**. The wheel shown includes the results of the further mixing of the primary and secondary colours to produce further, or tertiary, colours.

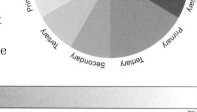

Harmonious colours are those that are close to each other on the colour wheel (for example, blue and green). **Complementary colours** are those that are opposite each other on the colour wheel (for example, red and green). These colours provide the greatest **contrast** to each other.

The colour itself is called the **hue**. The hue can be changed by adding tone – white to lighten it, black to darken it.

100%   0%

Colour Schemes

The use of a particular combination of colours is known as a **colour scheme**. Colour schemes usually consist of a number of various of hues and tones found in one part of the colour wheel, together with a small number of hues and tones found in the opposite side of the colour wheel.

Colour Association

Yellow, red and orange are known as '**warm**' colours. These colours are more noticeable. Blues and greens are known as '**cold**' colours and are much calmer.

People react emotionally to colour. For example, in the Western world red reminds people of danger and love. Green reminds them of safety, growth and nature. Other societies and religions sometimes have different responses to the same colours.

Colour Fusion

When small areas, or dots, of primary colours are placed together, the eye merges them together. Large advertising hoardings and TV images work on that principle. They are made up of millions of small dots that the eye 'reads' as a particular shape and colour. This is known as **colour fusion**.

Colour Separation

When printing a colour image, each colour is printed separately. A different printing plate needs to be produced for each colour. These are known as **colour separations**. A computer can generate these automatically.

Written Question

Answer the following question on plain paper. Do not spend more than 5 minutes writing your answer.

You have been asked to suggest a colour scheme for the packaging of a new flavoured milkshake drink. For each of the following flavours suggest two harmonious colours and one contrasting colour to be used on the outside of the container.

i)   Chocolate
ii) Strawberry
iii) Banana   *(6 marks)*

Presentation Media and Materials

Paper Work

Here's what you need to know...

about using a range of media and materials to present design ideas for graphic products.

See *Design & Make It! Graphic Products* Revised pages 42–43, 71 (34–35, 63 earlier edition).

KEYWORDS
Do you know what the following terms mean?
● Image library
● Encapsulation
● Multimedia

Designers use a variety of methods to help present their 2D graphic work.

Sometimes a series of images, graphs, charts and text are bound together into a booklet or folder. It's always a good idea to use standard sizes of paper and card.

Drawings and renderings can be mounted on to thicker card, both for impact and as protection against folding and tearing. Chalk and pastel work needs to be sprayed with a fixative to prevent it smudging. A transparent acetate sheet placed over the top of an image can be most effective.

Photography

Presentations often include photographs. These might be specially taken by the designer or found in an **image library**. Such photographs can be taken using traditional film and chemical printing. Alternatively, photographs can be created using a digital camera, enhanced on a computer and printed using laser or ink-jet technology.

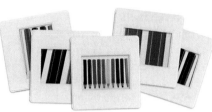

Lettering

Lettering can be created by hand, using a lettering stencil, or rub-down 'dry transfer' sheets. These days, however, most lettering is done on a computer.

Bringing it All Together

Elements included in a presentation, such as artwork, photographs, headings and text can each be created separately and 'pasted' together on to a background board. Alternatively, the composition can be done electronically on screen. The elements can be scanned or created directly on the computer and then combined together into one file. The presentation can then be printed out on to a single sheet.

Protection

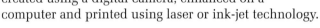

Some graphic products need to be handled by many people. Others need to be kept in good condition over a long period of time. These can be laminated with a protective plastic 'jacket'. This is called **encapsulation**.

Multimedia

As an alternative to being printed, the presentation might be created on the computer as a series of screens. As well as text and images, this could also include sound, animation and video. This is known as a **multimedia** presentation.

Written Question

Answer the following question on plain or lined paper.
Do not spend more than 5 minutes writing your answer.

A design team are preparing a presentation for local residents. The team will present their ideas for a new children's playground. They are preparing an A1 presentation board. List three presentation methods they could use, and suggest specifically what they might each be used to show. *(6 marks)*

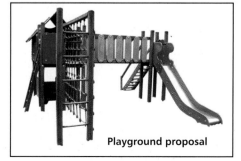

Playground proposal

Pictorial Drawings

Designers use a range of drawing techniques to show products and places in 3D. If the drawings are to be presented to a client or the public they need to be drawn very neatly using **technical drawing** aids such as set-squares, compasses, etc. or done on a computer drawing program.

Isometric

Isometric drawings are used to show what an object looks like in 3D. They are quite quick to draw, especially if isometric grid paper is used as an underlay. To create an isometric drawing you need to know what the plan and elevations of the object look like. The main things to remember are:

- lines that are vertical on the object are all vertical on the drawing.
- lines that are horizontal on the object are drawn at 30° to the left or right.
- circles and **ellipses** are drawn by using a stencil or template, or by first drawing a 'box' in which to fit the circle or ellipse.
- any 'hidden' lines need to be removed at the end.
- colour, shading and other **rendering** techniques can be added.

Planometric

A variation of isometric is called **planometric**. It is mainly used to help visualise room interiors or display stands. It differs in that the angles are drawn at 45° instead of 30°. This means that circular forms are easier to draw.

Perspective

Perspective sketches and drawings are similar to isometric drawings except that the lines appear to meet at the horizon at '**vanishing points**'. They are also more difficult to create.

There are two common types of perspective drawings, called '**one-point**' and '**two-point**'. The 'points' are the number of 'vanishing points' that the object recedes to.

- **One-point** perspectives are useful for views of simple objects or interiors.

- **Two-point** perspectives are useful for more complex products or room-interior drawings.

Here's what you need to know...

about using pictorial drawings such as perspective and isometric drawings.

See *Design & Make It! Graphic Products* Revised pages 108–109, 130–131 (100–101, 122–123 earlier edition).

KEYWORDS
Do you know what the following terms mean?
- Technical drawing
- Isometric drawing
- Ellipse
- Rendering
- Planometric
- Perspective

Written Question

Answer the following question on plain or lined paper.
Do not spend more than 5 minutes writing your answer.

Briefly describe the basic difference between perspective and isometric drawings. Refer to:
i)   their basic construction.
ii)   their level of difficulty.
iii)   their suitable application.   *(6 marks)*

Working Drawings

Working drawings are intended to enable someone other than the designer to make a product. For this reason they have to be clear and accurate. Various conventions and common **visual symbols** are used to help achieve this.

Orthographic Projection

In a working drawing 3D products are shown as a series of **plans** and **elevations**. The positioning on the drawing of these views follows a particular arrangement known as third angle **orthographic projection**. The plan is placed immediately above the front elevation. The side elevation is lined up to the left or right of the front elevation.

British Standards

The overall **dimensions** of the object or structures are drawn in a particular way, following a set of **BSI (British Standards Institute)** conventions (PD7308). In brief:

- dimension lines are placed to the side of the drawings.
- projection lines indicate the parts of the drawing the dimensions relate to.
- projection lines should not touch the drawing of the object or structure.
- dimension and projection lines should be half the thickness of the lines of the object or structure.

If a 2D **pictogram** is being drawn it should follow these same dimensioning conventions. Note that some **CAD** drafting programs use slightly different conventions, but you are expected to use British Standard conventions in the written paper.

There are other drawing conventions for working drawings, such as for drawing **cross-sections**, **cut-aways** and **exploded** views. Written information in the form of a table, or 'parts list', is provided to specify part numbers, materials and finishes and assembly instructions. Conventions for architectural drawings, such as site plans and maps, are very similar to, but slightly different from, those for objects.

Scale

Many drawings are drawn to **scale**, i.e. at a different size to the real object or structure.

A scale of 2:1 (i.e. twice normal size) might be used to draw a very small component.

In a drawing at a scale of 1:10, the drawing is one-tenth of the real, full size.

A scale of 1:500 might be used to draw a large public building.

Written Question

Answer the following question on plain paper.
Do not spend more than 10 minutes completing your answer.

Sketch out an orthographic drawing of the outline of the audio cassette box (15 × 70 × 110 mm) on the right, showing:
i)   a front elevation/view, an end elevation/view & plan.   *(3 marks)*
ii) three major dimensions to BSI (British Standards Institute) conventions.
                                                                 (3 marks)
iii) the BSI symbol for orthographic projection.   *(2 marks)*
iv) State the scale used.   *(2 marks)*

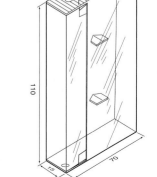

Surface Developments

Point-of-sale display stands are often made up from stiff, flat card or board, that is cut, folded and slotted together. The retailer often receives a point-of-sale display unfolded. This makes it easier and cheaper for the manufacturer to transport.

The shape of the card before it is folded up is called a **surface development** (or **net**). Below is the surface development of a simple six-sided box. Note where the flaps have been placed to provide a surface to take the adhesive.

Boxes and packages are assembled from surface developments (nets) to protect or enhance the contents, for example, an Easter egg box.

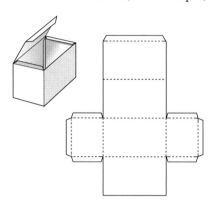

Tuck-in Boxes

Tuck-in boxes are those which include flaps and slots. When industrially made the corners of the tabs and flaps are **radiused** to smooth out the closing action.

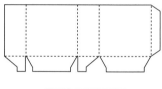

Automatic Bases

The bases of these boxes slot together very easily to speed up assembly. They are also known as '**crash-lock**' bases.

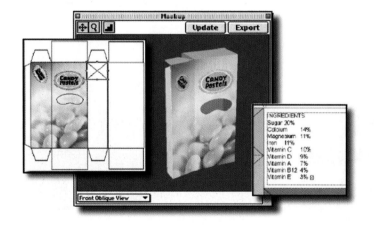

CAD-CAM

Surface developments (nets) can be created very effectively using **CAD/CAM**. A package can be designed on screen in 2D. The computer can then simulate what the surface development (net) will look like when folded up into 3D. The packaging graphics can also be applied to the 3D model.

When the surface development (net) has been finalised, its dimensions can be sent directly to a machine at the manufacturers that will cut the shape out, ready for **folding**. Some CAM machines have a **creasing** facility as well as a cutting tool.

Written Question

Answer the following question on graph or square grid paper.
Do not spend more than 10 minutes completing your answer.

A publishing company needs a counter-top point-of-sale stand to promote a new magazine. A sketch of the assembled design is shown on the right. It slots together, without the need for adhesive. Draw the surface developments (nets) of the two parts that make-up the stand. *(10 marks)*

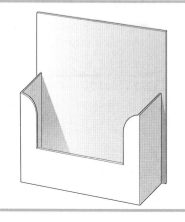

Information Drawings

Using Visual Images

Here's what you need to know...

about using drawings to communicate information graphically.

See *Design & Make It! Graphic Products* Revised pages 46–47, 82, 132–133 (38–39, 74, 124–125 earlier edition).

KEYWORDS
Do you know what the following terms mean?
- Visual symbol
- Logo
- Graphs and charts
- Flow charts
- Schematic

WWW.
Go to:
www.unece.org

Visual images often have great impact: they can be quickly remembered and recognised. They can also be understood just as quickly in different countries by people who speak foreign languages. However, the user still needs to have some understanding of the **conventions**, such as red meaning danger and a diagonal line meaning that this is something you can't do.

Signs and Symbols

Signs and symbols can often communicate **instructions** and **information** much quicker than words. Colour can also play an important part. Some **visual symbols** show movement. Others represent a product, place or service. Symbols can be entirely abstract – a shape or pattern.

Trademarks and Logos

There are two main ways in which companies and organisations identify themselves to the public. The first is to write their name in an unusual or distinctive style of lettering. The second is to use a visual symbol. In practice, many trademarks and **logos** use a combination of these two methods.

Graphs and Charts

Rows of numbers are often difficult to understand, and the relationships between them are not always obvious. Presenting data visually can help communicate such information easily and quickly. For example, the results of a survey can be shown as a **bar** or **pie chart**, or perhaps a **line graph**. A spreadsheet package can create these charts automatically.

Flow Charts

Production **flow charts** use 'labels'. The labels explain what needs to be happening at various stages of the making process. Some labels show that the product is being worked on, while others show if it is being moved, stored or inspected. Flow charts use standard symbols for various stages of the task, e.g. decision (diamond shape), process (rectangle), input/output (parallelogram), etc.

Maps

Schematic maps show the connections between places, but do not attempt to accurately represent the distances or geographical accuracy. They often use colours to show different routes.

Written Question

Answer the following question on plain paper. Do not spend more than 15 minutes completing your answer.

A new chain of magic shops called 'Hocus Pocus' is opening. You have been asked to design a corporate badge for its stationery and promotional items. To help you, the following specification has been provided:

- the words 'Hocus Pocus' must be included, but the letter style (font), size and colour(s) are up to you.
  (7 marks)
- there must be a magic-related image included in the design. It can either show a product the shop might sell, or be an abstract shape or pattern.
  (8 marks)

Annotate your design to explain your decisions.

The Quality of Design and Manufacture
Evaluating the Design and the Manufacture

When evaluating a graphic product, it is important to consider aspects of **design** and **manufacture**. A product might be well designed but badly made. Another might be poorly designed but well made. The best products will be well designed and well made.

A well-designed graphic product will:
● appeal to the needs and wants of particular **consumer groups**.
● efficiently perform the task it is intended to.
● be safe to use.
● be easy to clean and maintain.
● be simple to use.
● take environmental, social, moral and cultural **design issues** into account.

A well-made graphic product will:
● accurately fit together.
● have edges and surfaces that are well finished.
● be consistent in its quality.
● use materials and **components** that are appropriate for its intended use.
● accurately represent the intended manufactured product.
● work as well as the real product is intended to work.

Describing and Evaluating

Evaluating a product is not the same as **describing** it.

● To say that a product 'is 200mm wide and made in bright green plastic' is a *description* of it.
● To say that a product 'is 200mm wide to make it easy to use' goes a bit further. It *explains why* it is the way it is.
● To say that 'the bright green colour of the product successfully makes it attractive and appealing to young children' is an *evaluation* of the product. It says *how well* it works as a design.

When evaluating products try to use a range of suitable words such as: ***tightly*** fitting, ***harmonious*** colours, ***easy*** to use, ***difficult*** to open, ***hard*** to operate, ***fiddly*** controls, ***ingenious*** mechanism, ***sturdy*** construction, ***attractive*** shape.

Compare and Contrast

Where possible, try to **compare** and **contrast** the quality of the design and manufacture of the graphic product you are evaluating with another similar product.

● Comparing involves discussing things that are the ***same***. For example: This computer mouse is made from the same fashionable coloured transparent plastic as the more expensive one'.
● Contrasting involves discussing things that are ***different***. For example: 'This computer mouse fits the hand very comfortably, whereas this one has an awkward shape that makes it difficult to click'.

Written Question

Answer the following question on plain or lined paper.
Do not spend more than 5 minutes writing your answer.

Study the photograph of the graphic product shown on the right.

i) State three aspects you would consider if evaluating the quality of its design. *(3 marks)*
ii) State three aspects you would consider if evaluating the quality of its manufacture. *(3 marks)*

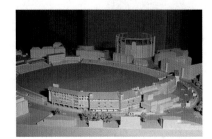

Investigating Needs and Wants

Developing New Designs

Evaluating existing products provides clues for possible new designs, based on modifications and improvements. The design of a new product is also likely to be developed from a detailed study of the changing interests and habits of potential **target markets**. This is done by doing a survey of current **market trends**. This provides information about how well existing products meet people's needs and wants.

Studying the sort of shapes and colours men now look for in an electric shaver identified the need for exciting new designs

Needs and Wants

There are certain things that people **need**, such as nutritious food, adequate clothing, warmth in winter, etc. There are also many things people **want** to make their lives more enjoyable, such as things that look good, are easy to use, do things more quickly, etc.

Do these products satisfy needs or wants?

Surveys

Conducting a **survey** does not involve obtaining information from everyone. Only a sample of the population from the target market needs to be studied.

Using a questionnaire, a sample is asked about their **lifestyle** – how they like to spend their time and money, what they would like to achieve, etc. Sometimes they are shown examples of existing products and asked how they think and feel about them – would they buy one, and if not, why not? Are they things they need or want?

From this information it is possible to predict what sort of products are most likely to appeal to certain types of people. Sometimes a '**gap in the market**' appears – a desired product that is not currently being manufactured.

Written Question

Answer the following question on plain or lined paper.
Do not spend more than 5 minutes writing your answer.

A market research company wants to find out whether a new magazine aimed at people interested in using alternative sources of energy in their homes would sell well. Briefly describe two ways in which it could attempt to discover if launching such a magazine would be a good idea. *(4 marks)*

Performance Requirements

Specification

Designers often study existing products to understand more about why products have been designed the way they have, and how they could be developed further.

When evaluating any product, a useful technique is to try and work out what the original **design** and **product specification** might have been, i.e. what the **performance requirements** (criteria) were. For example, if the cover of a child's book is bright red, the chances are that the original specification probably stated that primary colours were to be used.

Analysing 3D Graphic Products

Here are some of the questions a designer might consider when evaluating an existing 3D graphic product:

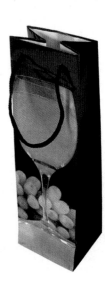

● What is the **target market**?
● Which **needs and wants** is it intended to satisfy? How well does it succeed?
● What are its performance requirements (e.g. speed, strength, capacity)? Could these be improved, or possibly reduced?
● What is its size and weight? Is it easy to handle in use?
● What is its **appearance**? Are the shapes, colours and textures likely to appeal to the target market?
● Is it **safe** to use? How effective are its safety features?
● What materials is it made from? Are they sufficiently **durable**?
● What **manufacturing** or **reproduction process** would have been used?
  What alternative methods might be considered to reduce time and costs?
● How many might have been made or printed? What variations in **batch size** (e.g. to produce different colours or models) could be introduced?
● How have **environmental** and **cultural issues** been addressed? Could these aspects be improved?

Analysing 2D Graphic Products

Here are some further questions a designer might consider when evaluating an existing 2D graphic product:

● Is the information easy to understand? Could the messages be made clearer?
● What **typefaces**, **illustrations**, **format** and **layout** have been used? What improvements might be made?

Written Question

Answer the following question on plain paper.
Do not spend more than 5 minutes completing your answer.

On the right is a picture of a drink's container produced ten years ago as a promotional product for a company. A design team are to be asked to develop a new, up-to-date version that will promote the company more effectively. List four design requirements for a new version, including references to function, materials and appearance.   *(4 marks)*

Testing and Evaluation by Designers

Approaches to Evaluation

Here's what you need to know...

about methods designers use to evaluate and test graphic products.

See *Design & Make It! Graphic Products* Revised pages 24–25, 53 and 91 (16–17, 45 and 83 earlier edition).

KEYWORDS
Do you know what the following terms mean?
● Performance test
● Personal opinion
● Quantitative
● Qualitative

WWW.
Go to:
www.usernomics.com/
meta.html
www.designcouncil.org/
betterbydesign

There are a variety of ways in which designs for graphic products can be evaluated. Some involve just the designer, which is what this section is about. Others need the help of other people, which is the subject of Study Guide 5.

The main evaluation approaches that a designer can use are:

● **performance tests**.
● **personal opinion and experience**.

Combining a range of different methods will provide a comprehensive evaluation of a product. The same methods can also be used to evaluate on-going design work.

Performance Tests

One way in which a design can be tested is to check out its performance – does it do what it says it will do, or at least what it is reasonably expected to do? For example:

● does a package hold as much as it says it will?
● does a 'pocket puzzle' fit in an average-sized pocket?
● how long does it take to replace the battery?
● does the 'crash base' of a food container always drop into place?
● is the take-away food container grease proof?

Such tests need to be set up in a **scientific** way, with numerical data being obtained. This information can be recorded in a spreadsheet and then presented as a graph or chart. This is known as '**quantitative**' evaluation. The results are a matter of **fact**, rather than opinion.

Personal Opinion and Experience

Another way to evaluate a design is to express a personal opinion – a bit like a review of a film or CD. As well as describing the design, comments on good and bad aspects need to be provided – what works well, and what might be improved.

A **user trip** or **user trial** can form a valuable part of such a test. The idea is to use the product in its intended circumstances and environment. At the same time the particular requirements of a typical user should be taken into account – perhaps someone who has never used such a product before, or maybe a disabled person who might find it difficult to hold or operate. This is known as '**qualitative**' evaluation. The results are a matter of opinion, rather than fact.

Written Question

Answer the following question on plain or lined paper.
Do not spend more than 10 minutes completing your answer.

You have been asked to evaluate a design for a pocket map for the neighbourhood in which you live. It includes information about public transport, local shops and businesses and other landmarks such as public buildings or parks. You decide to undertake a 'user trip'.

i)   Which particular design features of the map will you evaluate?   *(3 marks)*
ii) Say who the expected users are that you will be considering, and what their specific needs are.   *(6 marks)*

User Testing and Evaluation

Approaches to Evaluation

There are a variety of ways in which designs for graphic products can be evaluated. Some involve just the designer, which is what Study Guide 4 was about. Others need the help of other people, which is the subject of this section.

The main evaluation approaches that involve other people testing a product are:

● **user tests or trials**.
● **expert opinion**.

Combining a range of different methods will provide a comprehensive evaluation of a product. The same methods can also be used to evaluate on-going design work.

User Tests or Trials

In a user test, someone is asked to try a product out to see how well it works and how easy they find it to use. For example, can they work out how to use the instruction booklet to install and operate a new DVD player? The test needs to be tried by different people to take account of things such as previous knowledge and experience, physical size or disability, etc.

Here's what you need to know...

about how products can be evaluated by other people.

See *Design & Make It! Graphic Products* Revised pages 24–25, 53 and 91 (16–17, 45 and 83 earlier edition).

KEYWORDS
Do you know what the following terms mean?
● User tests or trials
● Expert opinion

WWW.
Go to:
www.usernomics.com/meta.html
www.designcouncil.org/betterbydesign

Expert Opinion

Another approach is to ask an expert. This might be:

● another designer or technologist with a particular area of expertise – for example, a materials engineer to comment on the choice of materials and finishes.
● a retailer, marketing or sales representative to advise on appearance and features.
● a representative of a relevant **consumer group** to comment on how well it meets particular **needs and wants**.

Written Question

Answer the following question on plain paper.
Do not spend more than 10 minutes completing your answer.

You have been asked to plan an evaluation of a new electronic bicycle speed/distance indicator.

i) Identify and describe a user performance test to evaluate the graphic instructions for fixing it on to the bike frame. *(3 marks)*
ii) Identify and describe a user performance test to evaluate the graphic controls and display for reading the speed/distance. *(3 marks)*
iii) Identify one type of 'expert' whose opinions could be sought, and say what they could be asked to comment on. *(3 marks)*

Social, Moral and Cultural Design Issues

Here's what you need to know...

about the social, moral and cultural design issues in graphic products.

See *Design & Make It! Graphic Products* Revised pages 6–7, 33 and 105 (25 and 97 earlier edition).

KEYWORDS
Do you know what the following terms mean?
● Social issues
● Cultural issues
● Moral issues

Social Issues

In Design and Technology, **social issues** can arise when a new product has an unforeseen side-effect on a group of people. This can be a good or a bad thing.

For example, the rise in use of mobile phones to send text messages has increased the demand for such phones. This:

● provides employment for factory workers.
● enables people to keep in touch more easily.
● means that there is less need for people to meet each other in person.

Cultural Issues

Cultural issues can arise when a new product does not take into account the fact that a particular shape, colour or name can have very different meanings to different groups of people.

Designers need to take care not to offend groups of people with different traditions and beliefs. For example, different cultures celebrate religious festivals in different ways.

An Easter Bunny chocolate egg.

A hand-painted hen's egg from the Ukraine.

However, a careful choice of name, shape and colour can help promote a sense of unity between different global cultures.

Moral Issues

Moral issues occur when a new product could help someone do something that might be considered undesirable or illegal.

For example, children enjoy playing with toy guns, but some people think that this encourages them to be more violent. So, designing a toy gun might raise moral issues.

Another example might be designing a poster that discouraged teenagers from taking dangerous drugs. This would be considered by the majority of people to be morally good.

Should children be stopped from playing with water pistols?

Written Question

Answer the following question using plain or lined paper.
Do not spend more than 10 minutes completing your answer.

i) Identify an actual graphic product you have in your home (e.g. a brochure, packaging, etc.). Briefly suggest what two of the social, moral or cultural issues might have been for the designer. (*5 marks*)

ii) Give a specific example of a situation in which a designer needed to consider social, moral and/or cultural issues. Explain how the designer responded. (*5 marks*)

Environmental Issues

Environmental issues are concerned with the impact a new product has on nature:

- a product may be made with a high proportion of materials that cannot be replaced, or use chemicals that **pollute** the atmosphere. This can also be harmful to wildlife and cause changes to weather patterns and the land.
- some production processes use high levels of **non-renewable energy**.

Paper and Wood

Paper and wood are made from trees. In many parts of the world forests are being destroyed. This is known as **deforestation**.

A high percentage of paper and wood can be used again if **recycled**, reducing the number of trees that need to be cut down. It is also important to ensure new trees are grown to replace the ones cut down through the use of **sustainable** forests.

Plastics and Metals

Plastics are made from oil and metals are mined from the earth. There are only limited supplies of oil and metal.

The amounts of plastic and metal used in a product need to be reduced to the minimum. Some plastics and metals can be recycled.

Decomposition

A product may be difficult to dispose of when it has been finished with. This can cause further environmental problems. An aluminium tin can take up to 100 years to **decompose**. Some materials, such as untreated paper and natural fabrics, decompose much more quickly. These are known as **biodegradable** materials.

Written Question

Answer this question using plain paper.
Do not spend more than 10 minutes completing your answer.

Sketch a simple two-colour design for a T-shirt to promote organic food. Your design should contain the words 'Have You Ever Bean Green?' and contain a visual image. *(10 marks)*

The 3 Rs

About the 3 Rs

When designing products it's important to remember the 3 Rs: **Reduce**, **Recycle** and **Reuse**. The 3 Rs provide guidance on how to minimise the damage a product does to the **environment**.

Reduce

Use the least amount of materials and energy when making a product.

Recycle

Use recycled materials and/or materials that can be recycled after use (e.g. untreated papers, glass).

Recycled materials are those which can be used again in new products. This usually involves separating the materials into different types and then cleaning and re-preparing them.

Reuse

Use products and **components** (e.g. containers, electronics, fastenings) that have already been used and/or can be used again in different products.

Disadvantages

While these approaches help save the environment, the 3 Rs can bring disadvantages in terms of:

- increased costs of materials.
- manufacturing and recycling processes.
- products that may not perform as well as required.

However, many of the most successful designs manage to combine **environmentally friendly** issues with low-cost, quality production.

Written Question

Answer the following question on plain or lined paper.
Do not spend more than 5 minutes completing your answer.

Identify a specific graphic product (e.g. packaging or promotional material) in your home. Explain how the designer and manufacturer might have applied the 3 Rs to help make the product more environmentally friendly.   *(5 marks)*

Environmentally Friendly Packaging

Packaging and the Environment

Here's what you need to know...

about the use of environmentally friendly packaging.

See *Design & Make It! Graphic Products* Revised pages 65 and 68–69 (57 and 60–61 earlier edition).

KEYWORDS
Do you know what the following terms mean?
● Recycle
● Reduce
● Reuse
● CFCs

WWW.
Go to:
www.thebodyshop.com
www.incpen.co.uk

The environmental aspects of packaging are of particular concern in the design of graphic products. Here are some of the things packaging designers and manufacturers do:

● use simple materials such as **recyclable** paper and card instead of plastics.

● **minimise** the amount of materials used, particularly where the packaging will only be used once and then thrown away.

● **reduce** the size, shape and weight of the packaging to minimise transport costs.

Packaging designers also:

● provide refillable containers that can be **reused**.

● avoid packaging materials that have been chemically treated during their production (e.g. using **CFC** gases), or that will poison the ground when decomposing.

● reduce the number of separate parts to make the package easier to throw away.

Written Question

Answer the following question on plain or lined paper.
Do not spend more than 5 minutes writing your answer.

The photograph on the left shows a household cleaning product. Suggest three ways in which the manufacturer might have taken environmental issues into consideration in the design of the container. *(6 marks)*

Environmental Graphics
Recycling Symbols

There is a wide range of **graphic symbols** used to show the environmental make-up of a product and its packaging.

- Some show the amounts of **recycled** materials used and the treatment processes involved.

- Others help remind users to **dispose** of the product and its packaging in the most effective way.

- These symbols are often coloured **green**.

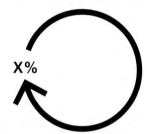

This is used across Europe to show the use of environmentally friendly packaging.

In Germany this symbol shows that the manufacturer has paid a fee towards the collection of the packaging after use.

This symbol shows the percentage of recycled matter used within the product or the material.

These both show that the packaging can be recycled after use.

Written Question

Answer the following question on plain paper. You will need some colouring pencils and pens. Do not spend more than 10 minutes completing your answer.

The photo on the right shows a plastic waste bin where people can place paper and card for recycling. A local council wants to order 1,000 of these in an appropriate colour and with suitable symbols. Prepare for the question by making a simple outline drawing of the bin on a piece of plain paper.

i) Show the position of an appropriate recycling symbol. *(2 marks)*

ii) Add an appropriate colour to the bin and a symbol. *(3 marks)*

Here's what you need to know...

about how CAD/CAM systems are set up for use in graphic products.

See *Design & Make It! Graphic Products* Revised pages 12–13 and 42–43 (34–35 earlier edition).

KEYWORDS
Do you know what the following terms mean?
● ICT
● CAD
● CAM
● CAD/CAM
● System
● Inputs
● Transform
● Outputs
● CNC

WWW.
Go to:
www.techsoftuk.co.uk

CAD/CAM Systems
Uses of ICT

In graphic products, **ICT** is often used to produce the following:
● working drawings
● package designs
● printed and electronically published materials
● patterns and moulds for 3D products

CAD/CAM Systems

CAD stands for Computer-Aided Design. **CAM** stands for Computer-Aided Manufacture. In a **CAD/CAM system**, **inputs** are **transformed** into **outputs**.

What You Put In

Inputs include elements such as text, data, photographs, graphic shapes and 3D forms. These are entered into the computer by means of keyboards, scanners and graphic tablets.

The inputs are transformed electronically within the computer. In other words, you can change the inputs using a computer program.

What You Get Out

The outputs are often print outs of text, data or images. These might be black and white or colour and produced on a laser or inkjet printer, or a plotter.

The outputs can also be in the form of information sent to another computer-controlled device, such as:
● a **profile cutter** to produce a stencil or template
● a **CNC** milling machine to produce the design in 3D.

Outputs can also be in the form of audio, video, multimedia CDs or web sites.

Milling Machines

There are three different types of **milling machines** that can be controlled by a computer.

A **2 axis miller** is a profile cutter. This means it can only cut out a **two-dimensional** shape. One axis is called X and the second is called Y.

A **2.5 axis miller** has an X and a Y axis, and a small Z axis. This means it can also undertake engraving and simple milling of sheet material.

A **3 axis miller** has fully controllable X, Y and Z axis adjustment allowing true **three-dimensional** cutting.

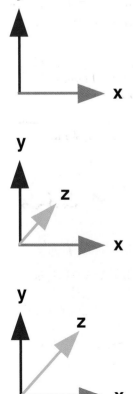

Written Question

Answer the following question on plain or lined paper. Do not spend more than 5 minutes writing your answer.

A designer is developing a new pop-up greetings card. State one input device, one type of computer program and one output device that might be used. State what each would be used for.

i) a) Input device
   b) Purpose
ii) a) Computer program
   b) Purpose
iii) a) Output device
   b) Purpose *(6 marks)*

Here's what you need to know...

about how 2D images can be created and manipulated using CAD to create graphic products.

See *Design & Make It! Graphic Products* Revised pages 11, 42–43, 139–142 (34–35, 131–134 earlier edition).

KEYWORDS
Do you know what the following terms mean?
● Electronic imaging
● Clip-art
● PhotoCD
● Vector graphic
● Bitmap graphic
● Desk-Top Publishing (DTP)
● Web page
● Digital transmission system

WWW.
Go to:
www.adobe.com
www.corel.com
www.macromedia.com
www.digitalvisiononline.co.uk

Using 2D CAD Programs
Electronic Imaging

Graphic work produced on a computer is sometimes called **electronic imaging**. First, the images to be used need to be entered into the computer. This can be done using a graphics tablet, a scanner or a digital camera. The image might already be in an electronic format, e.g. a piece of **clip-art**, on a **photoCD**, or downloaded from the internet. The image can then be worked on using a 'Draw' or 'Photopaint' program.

Draw programs produce what are called **vector** images. These produce files in which information about the start and finish of each line, together with its colour and thickness, is stored. Details of any colours used to fill shapes are stored as well. These files have quite small sizes.

Photopaint programs produce what are called **bitmap** images. These produce files in which information about the value of each pixel (e.g. position, colour, brightness) is stored. These have quite large file sizes.

It is sometimes possible to convert bitmap images into vector images, and vice versa. Many programs are able to work using both bitmap and vector images, e.g. **Pro/DESKTOP**, but the way of working with each type is slightly different.

Desk-Top Publishing

Another type of program often used in graphic product work is known as DTP, which stands for **Desk-Top Publishing**. In a DTP program, text, drawings and photographs can be brought together to create the layout for a brochure, magazine or book. The electronic files can be used to produce printing plates or to send data directly to a printer. One of the most common DTP programs used in schools is **Microsoft Publisher**.

Digital Presentation

Web pages and sites are created in programs in a similar way to DTP. The text and images are placed in a screen layout, and buttons added to link the different screens together.

'Presentation' programs can be used to create a series of computer-generated animated 'slide-show' screens for meetings and lectures. The most common presentation program used in schools is **Microsoft PowerPoint**.

Video and sound can also be entered into a computer, edited electronically and then output on to video tape, or directly to a **digital transmission system**.

Written Question

Answer the following question on plain or lined paper.
Do not spend more than 10 minutes writing your answer.

You have been asked to use a computer to design a leaflet to promote road safety in primary schools.
i) Identify three different sources of image you might use and say how these could be entered into a computer. *(6 marks)*
ii) Name a type of computer program you might use to create the leaflet. Give an example of a way in which you could use the program to develop the design of the leaflet. *(3 marks)*

Using 3D CAD Programs

3D CAD

3D CAD programs make it possible to create a **three-dimensional representation** of an intended product on screen. The image can be rotated in any direction, zoomed in and out, or 'walked round' to give an impression of what it would look like in reality.

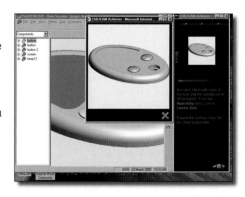

Modelling Methods

There are three main techniques involved:

- **Wire-frame modelling**, in which the object is seen on screen as a series of lines, or 'contours'. These models are not very realistic to look at but are quicker to rotate.
- **Surface modelling**, where colour, shading and texture are added to a wire-frame model to give a more realistic impression of what the object would look like. Different lighting sources can be set to highlight different parts of the product. These pictures can be printed out to create a '**virtual prototype**' to show to a client for approval, or for use in promotional material.
- **Solid modelling**, in which the geometry of the form shown on screen can be mathematically analysed by the computer. This can provide information on the way in which the object's mass, volume, etc., is likely to change in certain circumstances.

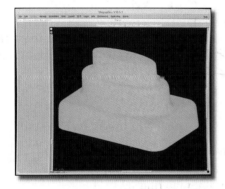

Rapid Prototypes

From these on-screen models it is possible to produce **rapid prototypes**. These are quick and cheap to produce. The data can be sent directly to a **CAM** machine that will make a 3D appearance model out of a solid block, or layered profiles, rather like a contour map.

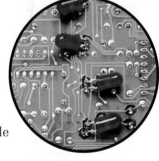

PCBs (Printed Circuit Boards)

Special software can be used to design electronic printed circuit boards. These can be printed out and used directly as masks to produce **PCBs**.

Other specialist programs and output devices are available for CAD/CAM work in textiles.

Written Question

Answer the following question on plain paper.
Do not spend more than 5 minutes completing your answer.

A team of designers is creating the casing for a new mobile phone. Name three applications of 3D CAD that could be suitably used in the design development process. For each, briefly explain their use and benefit.   *(6 marks)*

Sharing electronic data

Digital Transmission Systems

Before the widespread development of computer systems, all the artwork, working and instructional drawings needed to manufacture a product had to be put in the post or taken to the factory or printing works by the designer. This took time, and meant that the designer usually had to live within easy travelling distance.

Today things happen much faster. Using a **high-speed modem** connection, electronic artwork and drawings can arrive on the other side of the world in minutes. Sometimes data can be transmitted to instruct production machinery directly. With the right equipment it's easy to control and monitor a machine thousands of miles away.

Sending the Data

Electronic files need to be in the right **format** to ensure they can be understood by the CAM device. They may need to be **compressed** to reduce the amount of time it takes to send them, though this is less important if a high-speed modem is being used. Finally, it's important to check that the **e-mail address** of the receiver is exactly correct!

On the WWW

Web sites make it easy to access information stored on computers all over the world, if you know where and how to find it. This enables designers to become well informed about the latest research, technological developments and consumer trends.

Written Question

Answer the following question on plain or lined paper.
Do not spend more than 5 minutes completing your answer.

A designer has completed a design for a new pop-up book. It is to be printed and assembled outside the UK. All the page layouts, drawings and datafiles of the cut-out components exist electronically. Write a brief description of the stages and processes the designer would need to follow when sending his electronic files to the production works. Use the following words in your description (in any order):

format   compress   e-mail address   high-speed modem   *(5 marks)*

Using ICT

Advantages of Using CAD/CAM

Here's what you need to know...

about the advantages, disadvantages and implications of the increased use of ICT in the design of graphic products.

See *Design & Make It! Graphic Products* Revised pages 10–13, 119–120, 136–142 (111–112, 128–134 earlier edition).

KEYWORDS
Do you know what the following terms mean?
● 2D CAD
● 3D CAD
● CAD/CAM
● ICT
● Digital technology
● Global market

WWW.
Go to:
www.staedtler.co.uk

There are a number of important advantages and disadvantages in using **2D** and **3D** CAD/CAM. The main advantages are:

● **speed**, particularly in terms of experimentation and communication
● **accuracy** (i.e. fewer mistakes), particularly when things are copied
● **sharing** of data
● **ease** of storage and access
● increased **productivity**

Disadvantages of Using CAD/CAM

There are also a number of disadvantages.

● Computer technology is **expensive** to buy and maintain.
● Using computer technology requires a lot of **training** and experience.
● There is a lack of opportunity to experiment with real materials and 3D forms.
● It is easy to lose data if files are not regularly 'backed up'.

The Impact of ICT

ICT is having a significant impact on the way designers design, and the way we all live our lives. It means that in the workplace, the high street and the home things continue to change.

● New products can be created, modelled and changed far more quickly.
● Increased automation has produced higher quality products, but less work for the unskilled. Robotic devices can work in conditions that are unsafe for humans.
● The internet and other **digital technologies** now mean we can buy things from anywhere, without leaving our homes. As a result, many small local shops are going out of business.
● It is possible to access information and communicate with others much more quickly and easily, opening up **global markets**.

Written Question

Answer the following question on plain paper. Do not spend more than 10 minutes completing your answer.

a) Give three examples of when you used, or could have used, ICT in your Graphic Products course. Name the type of programs you used, or could have used, and state briefly what you did. *(6 marks)*
b) State two advantages and one disadvantage of using ICT over other methods when designing and making graphic products in school. *(3 marks)*

Consumer Information

Safety First

Designers and **manufacturers** have a responsibility to ensure that the products they provide are as safe as possible:

Components that might be dangerous, such as **electrical** parts, need to be safely contained within the product out of harm's way.

Here's what you need to know...

about recognising consumer information required by law, relating to graphic products.

See *Design & Make It! Graphic Products* Revised pages 89 and 104 (81 and 96 earlier edition).

- Materials need to be finished in such a way so that there are no sharp edges.
- Products must be **non-flammable**.
- Products must not become dangerous as they decay – e.g. leak chemicals or give off **poisonous fumes**.

KEYWORDS
Do you know what the following terms mean?
- Electrical
- Non-flammable
- Poisonous fumes
- BSI (British Standards Institute)

WWW.
Go to:
www.bsi.org.uk/education
www.incpen.co.uk

Safety Standards

All new products must conform to rigorous **BSI (British Standards Institute)** and European safety standards (and those that apply in other countries where the product may be sold). This includes the requirement to provide the consumer with necessary **safety information** and **warnings**.

Packaging Information

The packaging of a product needs to contain the name and address of the manufacturer, and any other information needed to help protect the **consumer**.

Pre-packed food must also include the ingredients, weight, sell by date, etc. The requirement to include nutritional information is voluntary, unless special health claims are being made about the product.

Other information often included is related to protecting the environment, materials used and product information sources.

Written Question

Answer the following question on plain or lined paper.
Do not spend more than about 3 minutes writing your answer.

A designer is preparing the packaging for a chocolate manufacturer's range of Easter eggs. The egg will include a chocolate bar that contains nuts, and a small plastic toy. It is aimed at children over the age of three years.

Identify three examples of health and safety information that will need to be included on the packaging to meet legal requirements. *(3 marks)*

Here's what you need to know...

about identifying quality assurance symbols and signs.

See *Design & Make It! Graphic Products* Revised pages 89 and 104 (81 and 96 earlier edition).

KEYWORDS
Do you know what the following terms mean?
● Quality assurance
● Visual symbol
● BSI (British Standards Institute)

WWW.
Go to:
www.bsi.org.uk/education

Quality Assurance Symbols
Making a Product Safe to Use

People like to know that the products they buy are safe to use. A manufacturer achieves this through their **quality assurance**.

A range of **visual symbols** have been designed to help consumers recognise instantly that the product they are buying conforms to the necessary safety standards. Some relate to **BSI** (British Standards Institute) specifications, others to European standards.

Here are some common examples:

The kite mark
This symbol confirms that the product complies with the requirements of the BSI (British Standards Institute). The product needs to be independently tested, and must be re-tested at regular intervals.

The CE mark
The letters CE show that a manufacturer claims that the product meets the essential safety requirements of the European Commission.

The e mark
This indicates that the contents of a package contain on average the quantity stated. The mark must be at least 3mm high and placed near to the quantity details.

Age warning
This symbol must appear on a toy (or its packaging) not suitable for children under 3 years old. The warning may be given by written words instead.

Written Question

Answer the following question on plain or lined paper.
Do not spend more than 5 minutes writing your answer.

The kite mark and CE mark are common examples of safety standard symbols. Give a brief explanation of the different meanings they have.

(4 marks)

Recognising Hazards and Assessing Risks

Making it Safe to Make

Here's what you need to know...

about using information to recognise hazards and assess risks when creating a graphic product.

See *Design & Make It! Graphic Products* Revised pages 89 and 104 (81 and 96 earlier edition).

KEYWORDS
Do you know what the following term means?
● Cumulative risk

WWW.
Go to:
www.bsi.org.uk/education

A manufacturer must consider the welfare of the people it employs to make the products, as well as ensuring that products are safe for the consumer to use. There are various **legal requirements** and **guidelines** to follow. These help reduce the risk of an accident happening.

Risk Assessment

The different steps and stages in a production process need to be identified as being high, medium or low risk operations. This is known as **risk assessment**. Appropriate levels of safety warnings and checks can then be allocated.

Most serious accidents happen when a number of normally safe individual events combine together. This is known as **cumulative risk**. For example:

● waste paper in a bin is not a hazard, unless a fire starts.
● a computer screen is not a health risk, unless you look at it for long periods without a break.
● spray paints are not harmful, unless you suffer from asthma.

Signs and Symbols

One of the most common ways of helping make the workplace safer is to use **signs** and **symbols** to warn employees of potential dangers. Symbols can also remind employees to follow safety procedures.

Colour Coding

● High-risk danger signs and symbols tend to be bright yellow, usually with black lettering. Yellow and black are the most noticeable combination of colours.
● Signs with red circles are mostly prohibitive. Diagonal lines are sometimes used to make it clear that this is something that must not be done.
● Signs with blue circles or rectangles are used to give positive instructions.
● Warning or caution signs are generally triangular.
● Green signs or symbols are often used to indicate where things are.

Safety in School

Safety procedures and risk assessment are important in school workshops, studios and classrooms too. You need to comply with **safety rules**. You also need to apply your knowledge of safety to your individual working situation to ensure your own safety and the safety of others. For example:

● recognise the dangers of bladed tools (knives, scalpels, etc.).
● know to open windows/ventilation when spraying paint or adhesive.

Written Question

Answer the following question on plain paper.
Do not spend more than 10 minutes completing your answer.

On the right is a symbol that reminds people to wash their hands. Using a similar style, design a symbol that advises that the tap water is not suitable for drinking. Only one colour may be used. No words can be included. The symbol is to be drawn inside a 50mm diameter circle. *(10 marks)*

Controlling Risk
Using Tools and Equipment Safely

Here's what you need to know...

about taking steps to control risk.

See *Design & Make It! Graphic Products* Revised pages 89 and 104 (81 and 96 earlier edition).

KEYWORDS
Do you know what the following terms mean?
● Safety precautions
● Safety warnings

WWW.
Go to:
www.bsi.org.uk/education

Workshops and studios can be dangerous places. There are lots of tools and equipment that can cause a great deal of harm if **safety precautions** are not followed.

It's important to think about the tools and equipment you use and the space you use them in. This section focuses on controlling the tools and equipment safely. Study Guide 5 looks at the spaces they are used in.

Using Power Tools

A model-making workshop will probably include a variety of electrically-powered drills, small lathes and hand-held tools. All these are potentially dangerous if mishandled. Always stop to think about the specific **safety warnings** your teacher has given you for each one. Also remember the general workshop rules that need to be observed.

Using Hand Tools

Even if you are only working in card or other graphic media there are possible hazards to be aware of. Adhesives, spray paints, craft-knives and even scissors can cause injury if not used with **caution**.

Using ICT

Remember too that there are safety considerations involved when using **ICT**. Never open the computer casing – there are high voltage currents inside. If you use computers for long periods you may start to suffer from backache, eye-strain or aching arms. Remember to take a break!

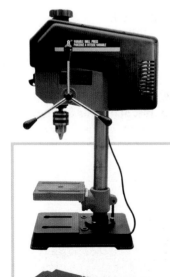

Written Question

Answer the following question on plain or lined paper.
Do not spend more than 10 minutes completing your answer.

i)   On the left is a photograph of a desk-top drill and a craft-knife. Identify two important safety requirements to remember when using each tool.   *(4 marks)*

ii) Briefly describe the potential health risks involved in working at a computer screen for long periods of time. Give three possible symptoms and state the most likely cause of each.   *(6 marks)*

Creating a Safe Working Environment

The Working Environment

Workshops and studios can be dangerous places. There are
lots of tools and equipment that can cause a great deal of
harm if **safety precautions** are not followed.

It's important to think about the tools and equipment you
use and the space you use them in. Study Guide 4 focused
on the tools and equipment. This study guide looks at the
spaces they are used in.

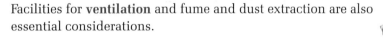

Placing Tools and Equipment

Careful planning of the layout of workshops and studios can
help reduce the risks of injury. Positioning some tools and
equipment close together can be **dangerous**.

For example, placing a computer next to a sink would not be
a wise idea as it might easily lead to **electrocution**.

The placing of power points and trailing cables also needs close attention.

Storage systems need careful thought. Is it easy to reach dangerous items? Are any
large piles of a material likely to fall over?

Maintaining the Air Quality

Facilities for **ventilation** and fume and dust extraction are also
essential considerations.

Dangerous fumes can be given off when plastic based products
are cut, or when two chemical components are mixed.

Adhesives, spray paints and varnishes can be dangerous if
inhaled.

Fine dust from cut materials can also be a problem if not extracted.

Looking After Yourself

Protective clothing, such as goggles, ear protectors and
overalls, needs to be readily available. Facilities for regular
washing are also necessary.

Written Question

Answer the following question on plain or lined paper.
Do not spend more than 5 minutes completing your answer.

i)   Describe two steps you took to control the risks involved at
     different stages of the making of your final coursework project.
     (2 marks)

ii) Identify two important safety considerations when planning the
     layout of a model-making workshop.   *(2 marks)*

System Breakdown

About Systems

Here's what you need to know...

about identifying input, process, output and feedback in the production of graphic products.

See *Design & Make It! Graphic Products* Revised pages 78–80 (70–72 earlier edition).

KEYWORDS

Do you know what the following terms mean?
● Control system
● System
● Inputs
● Outputs
● Feedback

Modern manufacturing and reproduction processes use complex **control systems** to operate quickly and reliably. A **system** is made up of a number of parts. In a well-designed and maintained system all the parts continuously work together in the most efficient way. In a poorly designed system a failure in one part can cause a major disruption to the whole system.

From Inputs to Outputs

All systems have **inputs**. These inputs are '**transformed**' or 'processed' into **outputs**.

In the production of a DVD package, the 'inputs' are a plastic box, a white paper insert, some printing inks and a printing plate. The transformation process involved is the inks being applied to the paper and the printed paper being added to the plastic box. The finished package is the 'output'.

Feedback

While the inputs are in the process of being transformed into outputs it's important to monitor the system. This is to make sure it's working properly. Information about the state of the system, such as whether there is enough paper or ink, is known as **feedback**.

In Control

As a result of the feedback the system can be controlled to keep it running smoothly – for example more paper can be loaded in, or more ink added. **Displays** (e.g. a warning light) and **controls** (e.g. a dial) help make this easier.

Written Question

Answer the following question on plain or lined paper. Do not spend more than 5 minutes writing your answer.

i) Name the three main parts of any system. *(3 marks)*

ii) Give an example of each main part of the system involved in the reproduction of a computer-generated colour poster for a school play. *(3 marks)*

Here's what you need to know...

about producing a flow chart of a system.

See *Design & Make It! Graphic Products* Revised pages 78–82 (70–74 earlier edition).

KEYWORDS
Do you know what the following terms mean?
- Flow chart
- Inputs
- Outputs
- Feedback

System Flow Charts

Flow Charts

A system can be drawn using a **flow chart**. This identifies the **inputs** and **outputs** and shows the different stages of a sequence of events. It can also show where **feedback** occurs. Different **symbols** are used to show different parts of the process. The symbols are linked together by **arrows**. These show that one event follows on from another. The aim is to make the flow chart as simple to follow and understand as possible.

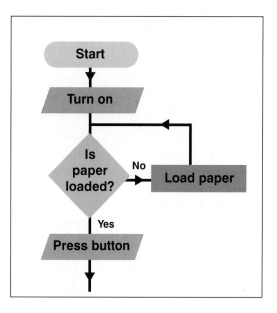

In Production

When planning a **production line**, a slightly different set of symbols are used. In a complicated product, each stage of manufacture would have its own flow chart, with a master chart showing how the stages all flow together.

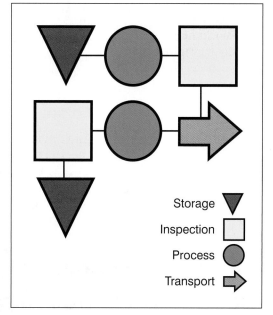

Written Question

Answer the following question on plain or lined paper. Do not spend more than 10 minutes on your answer.

You are about to make a full-size card prototype of a point-of-sale unit.

i)   Rearrange the production stages listed on the right into the correct order.   *(4 marks)*

ii) Place the stages into a flow chart using appropriate symbols.   *(4 marks)*

Start

Crease the edges

Glue the tabs

Add graphics

Assemble unit

Cut out

Mark out development (net)

Check shape and size

End

Registration Marks and Colour Bars

Checking Proofs

Here's what you need to know...

about how registration marks and colour bars are used to provide feedback in the production of graphic products.

See *Design & Make It! Graphic Products* Revised pages 88–89 (80–81 earlier edition).

KEYWORDS
Do you know what the following terms mean?
- Feedback
- Production run
- Proof
- Registration
- Colour reproduction

When graphic products are being printed there are a series of checks to be undertaken. This provides **feedback** (i.e. information), that is used to make adjustments to the printing presses. This ensures that each print is of the correct quality.

Before the full **production run** is undertaken a number of **proofs** will be checked for accuracy. Further checks are then made to maintain the quality throughout the run.

Registration

One fault that can occur is in the **registration**. Colour reproduction involves printing different colours on top of each other. If they are not exactly on top of each other the image will look blurred.

To quickly ensure that the printing plates are correctly aligned, the 'registration mark' is checked. This is printed on the area of each print that will be later trimmed off. If it is correct the mark will appear as fine black lines. If it is not correct one or more coloured lines will appear offset from the mark.

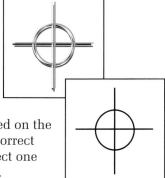

Colour Accuracy

Another fault can be in the accuracy of **colour reproduction**. This can be quickly checked on the **colour bar**, which is also printed on the area to be trimmed.

Each of the print colours (yellow, magenta and cyan) are printed at different **densities** (typically 20%, 40%, 60%, 80% and 100%) which can be easily compared.

The black and grey bars provide a useful check, as they will appear coloured if the print colours are not properly balanced.

黑色 BLACK

An experienced colour proofreader can spot inconsistencies by eye, but there are also electronic devices, such as a **densitometer**, that can be used.

The printer will also check many other elements such as poor reproduction of type.

Written Question

Answer the following question on plain paper.
Do not spend more than 5 minutes completing your answer.

Two methods used to provide feedback on the quality of colour prints are registration marks and colour bars.

i) Explain how a registration mark is used to check print quality. *(3 marks)*
ii) Explain how a colour bar is used to check print quality. *(3 marks)*

Simple Mechanisms

Mechanical Systems

Mechanisms are examples of **systems**. The **input** is the energy used to move one component one way, and the **output** is the result, e.g. a different component moving a different way. Mechanisms transform (i.e. change) one type of motion into another type.

In graphic products mechanisms are mainly used in pop-up books and cards, or in unusual promotional materials.

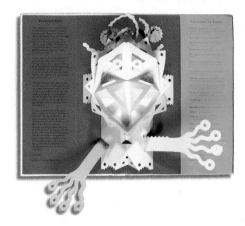

Types of Motion

There are four types of motion: **linear, reciprocating, rotary, oscillating**.

A pop-up book or card might use any of these types of motion to turn, push or pull different parts.

Linear motion
Linear motion is movement in a straight line.

Reciprocating motion
Reciprocating motion is a repeated backwards and forwards movement in a straight line.

Rotary motion
Rotary motion is a circular movement.

Oscillating motion
Oscillating motion is a repeated left to right/right to left movement that follows a curved path.

Cams

Cams can also be included in mechanisms. These can change a rotary motion into another type of movement.

1

2

3

4

Written Question

Answer the following question on plain or lined paper. Do not spend more than 5 minutes completing your answer.

On the left are drawings of four different mechanisms used in a pop-up book. Name the type of motion used in each. *(4 marks)*

Complex Mechanisms

Levers

A **lever** is a simple type of **mechanism**. It can magnify the push or pull force (the **input**) and changes the **direction of movement**, but not its type.

All levers consist of a **load**, **fulcrum** (or pivot) and an **effort**. These can be in different positions. Finding the correct position for the pivot is very important.

Levers are found in many everyday products such as seesaws, scissors and wheelbarrows, and in pop-books and cards.

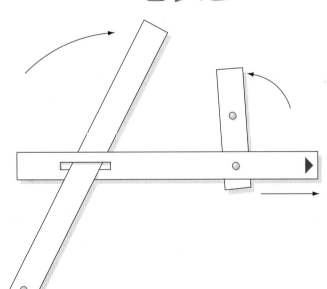

Linkages

When two or more levers are joined together, it is called a **linkage**. It is possible to connect two levers to move in opposite directions at the same time. Some pop-up mechanisms link different combinations of types of lever together.

Written Question

Answer the following question on plain paper.
Do not spend more than 10 minutes completing your answer.

i) Name the three parts of a lever. *(3 marks)*

ii) On the left is a sketch of a design for the front of a promotional card to be used to promote a new health drink. When the tab on the right is pulled the athlete's arm will raise the bottle to his mouth.

Produce a sketch of the reverse side of the card to show the lever mechanism that would be needed. *(3 marks)*

iii) Mark the positions of the three parts of the lever. *(3 marks)*

Here's what you need to know...

about the different methods of quantity production of graphic products.

See *Design & Make It! Graphic Products* Revised pages 23, 81–85 (15, 73–77 earlier edition).

KEYWORDS
Do you know what the following terms mean?
- One-off production
- Batch production
- Production run
- Mass production
- Continuous production
- Just in Time (JIT)

Quantity Production
Making Things in Quantity

The number of products that need to be made has an effect on the way they will be made. The steps and stages involved differ according to the **method of production** being used. Sometimes the design may need to change to suit the production method.

One-off production

One-off production

One-off production is when just one product is made. There are very few one-off products as they are very expensive. A mural or a specially painted poster would be an example of a one-off graphic product. Other examples include film and theatre sets, trade show stands. An architectural model or industrial prototype of a proposed design could also be described as a one-off.

Batch production

Batch production is when a specific number of products are made. Most graphic products are produced in batches, called **production runs**. For example, 5,000 brochures or posters might be printed. The printing press would then be reset to print a different product.

Other examples include newspapers and magazines, food packaging, CD sleeves and inserts, commemorative postage stamps, business cards, letterheads and graphics for lorries and vans.

Batch production

Mass production

Mass production

Mass production is when a production line is only used for the manufacture of one product in very large quantities. Production continues until there is no longer any demand. A motor car is a good example of a mass production. Very few graphic products are mass-produced, but examples might include standard packaging designs for food products such as cornflakes and milk cartons, and standard postage stamps.

Continuous production

Continuous production is when a mass production line never stops working. Very few products are made in this way. Chemical works, steel manufacture, newsprint (the paper newspapers are printed on) and industrial bread making are some examples.

Continuous production

Just In Time

On a production line, the term **JIT**, or **Just In Time** is used to describe a production line where the materials and component parts arrive at the processing equipment as close as possible to the time they are needed. Using a 'just in time' approach reduces manufacturing costs by cutting warehouse charges, preventing over-ordering and stocking unwanted components. However, if the supply of materials and components fails and production stops, it can be very costly to restart.

Written Question

Answer the following question on plain or lined paper. Do not spend more than 10 minutes writing your answer.

a) Name the four methods of production.
(4 marks)

b) Match the following products to the most appropriate production method. Give a reason for the choice of each method:
   i) a weekly magazine
   ii) a hand-painted shop name sign. *(4 marks)*

c) What do the initials JIT stand for? *(2 marks)*

Commercial Printing Methods

There are five main methods of printing:
● Letterpress
● Lithography
● Gravure
● Flexography
● Screen printing

The method chosen depends on the length of the **print run**, the **quality required** and the **cost**.

Letterpress

Letterpress is a form of **relief** printing. Each letter is raised from the surface and ink applied to it. Although the quality of text produced can be extremely high it is expensive, and only suitable for short runs.

Lithography

In **lithography** a plate is made that has areas that **attract** ink and other areas that **repel** ink. This is a popular method of printing that is economical for medium and long print runs of magazines, posters and packaging.

Gravure

Gravure involves the production of an etched plate on to which ink is poured. It is used for very high quality long run print work, such as stamps or expensive magazines and illustrated books.

Flexography would have been used to print the colours on top of this embossed tin lid

Flexography

Flexography uses a plastic or rubber relief plate. This method is used for printing on to unusual surfaces such as plastic bags, corrugated card and wallpaper.

Screen Printing

Screen printing uses a **stencil** through which ink is forced. This method is low-cost and only suitable for short print runs. Fine detail is not possible, but it is effective at producing bright colours and bold shapes. It can be used for posters, T-shirts and large shop display boards.

Written Question

Answer the following question on plain or lined paper.
Do not spend more than 5 minutes writing your answer.

Match the following graphic products with the most suitable industrial printing method. Give one reason why your chosen printing method is suitable.

i) A school textbook.
ii) The graphics on a plastic bottle.
iii) A reproduction of a work of art.

(6 marks)

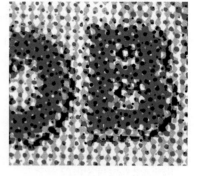

Process Colours

Printing in Colour

A typical colour printing press uses three different coloured printing inks, and black. The printing inks are **cyan**, **magenta** and **yellow** (cyan is a shade of blue and magenta is a shade of red). By printing different amounts of each colour in different sized dots on to a roll of paper, any colour can be produced. The eye combines the dots to give the illusion of the mixed colour. This is known as **colour fusion**.

The four printing colours are called **process colours**. They are also represented by the initials **CMYK**, which stands for Cyan, Magenta, Yellow and Black (represented by the letter K which stands for Key image).

Colour Separation

To achieve this the image must be separated into four different printing plates – one for each of the process colours. This is known as **colour separation**.

Each plate covers the area to be printed in that particular colour, and holds the amount of ink required. For example, to produce an orange colour a surface needs 0% Cyan, 45% Magenta and 100% Yellow. Turquoise is made up from 100% Cyan, 40% Magenta and 15% Yellow. These colour separations are now done automatically by a computer.

Although 100% Cyan, 100% Magenta and 100% Yellow combine to produce black, a separate black ink is also used to add contrast and print any black outlines.

On the Spot

Some presses have more rollers that include **special inks** (e.g. silver ink) for particular effects, or for particular areas of block colour. These are known as **spot colours**.

Order of Printing

Black is usually printed first, as it tends to have the lightest coverage. Cyan and Magenta follow. Yellow, which usually has the heaviest coverage, is printed last.

Written Question

Answer the following question on plain or lined paper.
Do not spend more than 10 minutes completing your answer.

i)   Name the four process colours.   *(4 marks)*
ii) Explain briefly how these four colours are able to produce a full-colour image when printed.   *(4 marks)*

Special Effects

In addition to the basic print process there are a range of **special graphic effects** that can be created. The three most common are:

- varnishing
- laminating
- embossing

Other special effects can include the use of metallic papers and inks, and holographic images. Specifying special printing effects can add considerably to the cost of the **print run**.

Varnishing

Varnishing is the addition of a thin glossy finish to protect the printed surface, and make it look more attractive. There are four main types of varnish:

- **oil-based**
- **water-based**
- **ultra-violet**
- **spirit-based**

Spot varnishing is where only a particular area of the surface is varnished. This provides a contrast between the varnished and matt areas.

Laminating

Laminating is the addition of a thin plastic coating to achieve a **high-gloss finish**. Laminating is significantly more expensive than varnishing, but does provide better protection and quality of finish.

Laminating should not be confused with **encapsulation**. This is a completely different process in which a document is placed inside a pre-gummed transparent plastic envelope and sealed inside.

Embossing

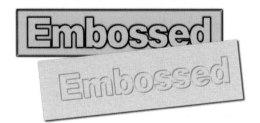

Embossing is where part of the surface of the paper or thin card is raised slightly to give a three-dimensional effect. This can make a printed surface of a package or a book cover much more distinctive and interesting. Each sheet needs to be pressed over a **steel die** that carries the required shape.

Written Question

Answer the following question on plain or lined paper.
Do not spend more than 10 minutes completing your answer.

i) Name the four main types of varnish used in print products. *(4 marks)*

ii) Compare and contrast the similarities and differences between varnishing and laminating. *(4 marks)*

Here's what you need to know...

about cutting and folding tools used in the production of graphic products.

See *Design & Make It! Graphic Products* Revised pages 76–77 (68–69 earlier edition).

KEYWORDS
Do you know what the following terms mean?
- Guillotine
- Die cutter
- Jigs
- Creasing bars

Cutting and Folding Tools

Cutting to Shape

In industry large sheets of printed paper are cut into rectangular shapes using a **guillotine**. Specially shaped **die cutters** are used to stamp out irregular shapes.

Shaping and Folding

Many printed products require **folding**: to make a book, leaflet or magazine, for example. This is usually done automatically at high speed. Special machines are used that can trim, crease and fold the paper.

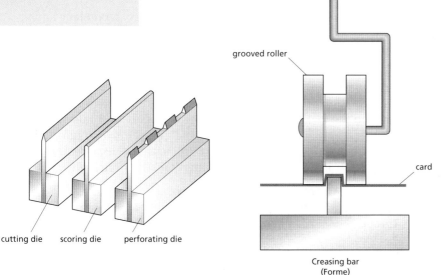

cutting die   scoring die   perforating die

grooved roller

card

Creasing bar
(Forme)

Creating irregular shapes or folds greatly increases the cost of a printed product, and takes longer to produce. Special tools or **jigs** may need to be made. However, the impact of a non-rectangular shape makes the product very distinctive.

Creasing bars are used to form a shaped recess along which a fold is later easily made. Die cutters and creasing bars will be specially made for the requirements of each product, and then used again if it is reprinted.

Cutting in School

In school large sheets of paper can be accurately cut on a **rotary trimmer**. A rotary trimmer is not very good at cutting thick card material or many sheets of paper at once, however.

Written Question

Answer the following question on plain paper.
Do not spend more than 5 minutes completing your answer.

A designer is creating a promotional leaflet that will have a simple pop-up feature in it.

i)   Name two special tools that are likely to be needed to produce irregular shapes and folds during manufacture.   *(2 marks)*
ii) Give two disadvantages of the need to use these tools.   *(2 marks)*

Here's what you need to know...

about the function and purpose of packaging.

See *Design & Make It! Graphic Products* Revised pages 58–59, 64, 68–69 (50–51, 56, 60–61 earlier edition).

KEYWORDS
Do you know what the following terms mean?
• Primary packaging
• Secondary packaging
• Tertiary packaging

WWW.
Go to:
www.thebodyshop.com
www.incpen.co.uk

Packaging

Packaging Matters

Packaging is an essential part of the manufacturing process. It helps ensure that the products being made end up arriving in the **retailer's** shop or warehouse and the **consumer's** home or workplace in the same condition in which they left the factory.

Products need to be contained so that they:
• are protected from damage, theft or contamination.
• can be quickly identified.
• are easy to carry and transport.
• can be stored safely until needed.

Packaging serves to contain things that are:
• **perishable**, such as food and drink.
• **dangerous**, such as chemicals.
• **precious**, such as jewellery.
• **numerous**, such as the parts of flat-pack, self-assembly furniture.
• **liquid**, such as shampoo, fragrances, motor oils.

Levels of Packaging

There are three main levels of packaging, known as **primary**, **secondary** and **tertiary**.

Primary
This type of packaging is used to protect the product from damage and pilfering, and to provide information about handling, storage and the enclosed contents.

For example, a brown corrugated cardboard box containing one large item such as a TV, stereo system, or refrigerator, or several smaller boxed items such as tinned goods, cornflakes, bottles, etc.

Secondary
This describes the immediate package containing the product. This is usually thinner card of a better quality. It is frequently highly decorated showing the item and giving detailed information to the purchaser, e.g. legal requirements, assembly instructions, safety warnings.

Tertiary
This describes any final protective covering, e.g. sweet wrappings, plastic bags holding small components.

Packaging Design

Secondary packaging is often used to help **sell** the product. Eye-catching graphics need to draw people's **attention** to the product on the shelves and make it look **desirable**. At the same time it must not give a misleading impression of the contents of the package.

Written Question

Answer the following question on plain or lined paper. Do not spend more than 15 minutes writing your answer.

A supermarket is to introduce its own range of luxury chocolates. You have been asked to prepare an outline design specification for the box.

i) Give three reasons why packaging is necessary for this type of product. *(6 marks)*

ii) a) Give two examples of what a customer might look for in a box when buying luxury chocolates in a supermarket. *(2 marks)*

b) Give two examples of what the chocolate manufacturer will require from a brown corrugated board box containing 24 boxes of luxury chocolates. *(2 marks)*

iii) List two materials commonly used in the packaging of chocolate products, and explain the purpose of each. *(4 marks)*

iv) Give two types of information about the chocolates that will need to appear on the outside of the package. *(2 marks)*

Barcode Scanning

Barcode Information

All product packages or labels now carry
barcodes. At the **point-of-sale** these save
the till operator from having to type in the
name of the product and its price. However,
barcodes also provide the **retailer** with a
great deal of useful information about:

● where the item has come from.
● where different items are in the warehouse, and in what quantities.
● how different product lines are selling, and which ones need reordering.
● what other things the customer purchased at the same time.

As well as keeping the shelves fully stocked, this information is also used to
provide useful marketing information about customers' shopping habits and
preferences.

Barcoding Systems

There are a number of different **barcoding systems**. They all use a series of black
strips of different widths, and spaces between them. A **laser beam** scans the strips
and records the line widths as pulses, which it converts into a numerical value. The
patterns are created automatically by a computer program.

Most barcode numbers contain three items of information:

● the first two numbers show the country of origin.
● the next five numbers show the manufacturer's reference
number.
● the next five numbers show the specific product number.

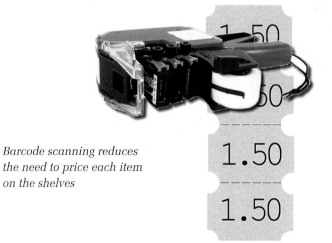

*Barcode scanning reduces
the need to price each item
on the shelves*

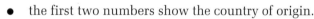
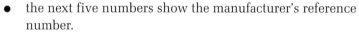

Written Question

Answer the following question on plain or lined paper.
Do not spend more than 5 minutes writing your answer.

The inlay card for a CD contains a barcode. Describe
three advantages to the retailer in using a barcode
scanning system to collect information.   *(6 marks)*

Units of Paper and Card

Quantities of Paper

There are many different shapes, sizes and thicknesses of paper, card and board. These materials are sold by **size** and **weight**.

Size

There are many sizes of paper, card and board, but the most widely used is the 'A' series. This ranges from the largest A0, though A1 to the smallest, A6. Each size is half the size of the previous one. A4, which measures 297 x 210mm, is the most familiar.

Weight

There are also many weights, or thicknesses of paper. The unit of measurement used is grams per square metre (known as **gsm**). A typical sheet of exercise paper is about 70gsm, while a good quality magazine cover may be more like 150gsm (i.e. just over twice as thick).

Thicker card and boards are sometimes sold in units called **microns**. A micron is one millionth of a metre. A standard card used for packaging might be around 350 microns.

Treated Papers

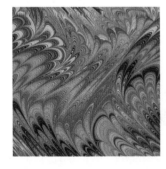

During manufacture, most paper, card and board is **treated in** some way to make it more suitable for a specific purpose:
- Sizing agents improve water resistance.
- More bleach can be added for extra whiteness, or the paper can be passed through highly polished rollers for a glossy appearance.
- Dyes provide colour and different mixtures of pulp create textured effects. Some papers and boards are made with higher proportions of recycled paper.
- Other papers have special finishes to make them more suitable for different printing applications, such as colour photos.

Paper can also be classified in terms of its:
- **durability** – how long it lasts.
- **brightness** – how well it reflects light.
- **texture** – how rough or smooth it is.
- **opacity** – how transparent it is.

Here's what you need to know...

about the different types of paper and card.

See *Design & Make It! Graphic Products* Revised pages 66, 71 (58, 63 earlier edition).

KEYWORDS
Do you know what the following terms mean?
- gsm
- Microns

WWW.
Go to:
www.severnprint.com/seve rnprint.html

Written Question

Answer the following question on plain paper.
Do not spend more than 10 minutes completing your answer.

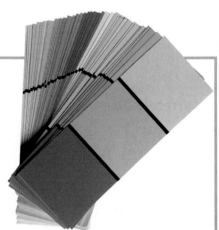

i) If a sheet of A4 paper measures 297 x 210mm, what is the measurement of a sheet of A3 paper? *(2 marks)*
ii) What does the abbreviation 'gsm' stand for? *(2 marks)*
iii) Name and describe three ways in which paper, card and board can be treated for a particular purpose. *(6 marks)*

Reducing Waste

The cost of a single sheet of paper or card may seem very cheap. However, when multiplied by many thousands the price starts to become more significant. Reducing the amount of wasted material by as little as 5 or 10% can save a great deal of money.

To help **minimise waste**, printed products are designed to fit the maximum amount of useful surface on to a sheet, or roll, of paper. For a standard book or magazine this means that up to 16 pages are typically printed on each side of one large sheet before being folded up and trimmed.

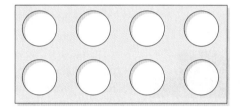

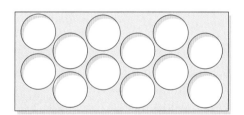

Tessellation

Sometimes an irregularly shaped **surface development** (or **net**) needs to be printed. The layout of the shape on each sheet must be carefully planned to maximise the number that can be produced. This is called **tessellation**.

A computer can be used to work out the most **cost effective** arrangement. Sometimes changes are made to the design of the surface development to increase the number that can be placed on the sheet.

Reducing Storage Space

Over-sized or irregular boxes take up more space than is really needed. This means less can be fitted on to a standard industrial pallet and lorry. In turn, this increases transport costs and wastes energy.

Written Question

Answer the following question on plain or lined paper.
Do not spend more than 5 minutes completing your answer.

The square opposite shows a sheet of board 1.5 × 1.5 metres. It is to be used to print parts of a point-of sale display unit.

Three identical nets have been marked out. Redesign the layout of the net and produce a sketch to show how they could be more effectively placed to increase the number that can be printed out. *(6 marks)*

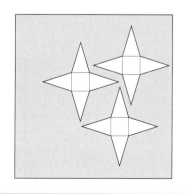

Here's what you need to know...

about using a range of devices to aid the production of graphic products.

See *Design & Make It! Graphic Products* Revised pages 62–62 (54–55 earlier edition).

KEYWORDS
Do you know what the following terms mean?
● Template
● Jigs
● Formers
● Creasing bar
● Mould
● Vacuum forming

Using Patterns, Templates and Jigs
Making It Quickly and Accurately

Manufacturers use a range of devices to help make production as quick and as efficient as possible.

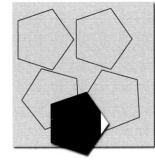

Templates

One of the simplest devices is a **template**. This is where a standard shape is repeatedly used as a **pattern** for cutting a series of identically shaped pieces. A lettering or circle stencil is a form of template.

Jigs and Formers

Jigs and **formers** are used to help accurately locate materials and components during manufacture. This saves time re-measuring a cutting, drilling or construction point on each part. In the construction of the card mechanisms for a pop-up book, specially shaped **creasing bars** and jigs might be used to locate small holes. These help ensure each part is identical and quick to make.

Die Cutting

Shapes in card can be created in a number of ways. The traditional way is to use a **hollow die**, which works in a similar way to a pastry cutter. These days, however, most cuts are made by **laser technology**, which is extremely sharp and precise, producing a highly accurate and clean cut.

Moulds

Moulds are used to produce identical copies of a 3D form. A softened material takes on the shape of the mould. When it hardens it is removed, leaving the mould ready to be used again. The **vacuum former** works on this principle, and is widely used in the production of packaging, e.g. 'blister' packs.

Written Question

Answer the following question on plain or lined paper.
Do not spend more than 5 minutes writing your answer.

Name two devices used by manufacturers to help make production as quick and as efficient as possible. State what each device is used for.   *(4 marks)*